Swiftly Flowing Waters

a memoir

A Métis woman's story of
resilience, reflection, and reclamation

For my daughter and granddaughter

— Pat Lamondin Skene

www.plumleafpress.com

Library and Archives Canada Cataloguing in Publication
xxx

24 25 26 27 28 5 4 3 2 1

ISBN 978-1-7388982-9-9

Printed in China

Cover Design: Karen Gold

Swiftly Flowing Waters

a Memoir

A Métis woman's story of
resilience, reflection, and reclamation

PAT LAMONDIN SKENE

Author Acknowledgement

I want to start by thanking my biggest cheerleaders, my daughter, Andrea, and granddaughter, Farrell, for their love and support. I appreciate the help from my family, especially Bruce, Ann, Maureen and Dave, for remembering the old stuff and for putting up with all my questions. I'm forever grateful to my niece Jessica for her relentless pursuit of our Métis roots and for setting me on the road to discovering my indigeneity. My sincere appreciation to author Maggie de Vries, who coached me in the early draft stages and taught me to dig deep. I'm grateful to Maggie Goh and the staff at Plumleaf Press for their insightful editorial input and beautiful cover design. I'd also like to acknowledge the input and support I received from the Métis Nation of Ontario and the Credit River Métis Council. And finally, I'd like to thank everyone mentioned in this book for being part of my story.

Disclaimer

This work depicts actual events in the life of the author as truthfully as recollection permits and/or can be verified by research. Some events have been compressed, and occasionally, dialogue consistent with the character or nature of the person speaking has been recreated. All persons within are actual individuals; there are no composite characters. The names of some individuals have been changed to respect their privacy. The words "Indian," "squaw," "half-breed," and "Indian reservation" are used in the historical context of the story.

Land Acknowledgement

As a resident of Oakville, Ontario, I acknowledge that this book was written on the traditional lands of the Mississaugas of the Credit, part of the Anishinaabe Nation that extends from the Niagara Peninsula across Hamilton, Halton, and Toronto to the Rouge River Valley. I acknowledge and thank the Mississaugas of the Credit First Nation for being stewards of this traditional territory. I also recognize the enduring presence of Indigenous people on the land and the waters that surround us. They reflect our histories and continue to teach important lessons every day.

CONTENTS

AUTHOR'S NOTE

In my dreams, I'm always thirty-two. I look thirty-two, I dress the way I did in the 1970s, and in my dream, when people ask how old I am, I tell them I'm thirty-two. I'm never the white-haired Métis grandmother I see flossing her teeth in the mirror the next morning. Some days, I look at my reflection and think ... *that can't be right.*

It took the profound experience of grief and coming face to face with the finality of death to make me think more deeply about the path I've been on. I'm not afraid of dying — it's the living and growing old that's the scary part. When I knit together my memories of the past seventy-plus years, I wrap myself in an image of who I was and who I came to be. Looking back, I sometimes wonder what it was all about.

My indigeneity has always been in the shadows of my backstory, running in parallel lines along the events of my life. I've come a long way from the prejudices of my early experiences, when I learned that I had "some Ojibwe" connection in my family. As a child, racism and discrimination were tolerated and expected, which kept Indigenous people, including Métis people, silent about their identity.

Throughout my life, despite not fully understanding who I was at my most central core, I have always had an Indigenous way of being and seeing the world. My love of water, my joy of storytelling, my connection to family, and my appreciation of Indigenous art have always been part of who I am. It's been a long journey from hearing the words "squaw" and "half-breed" to self-identifying as Métis and becoming a proud citizen of the Métis Nation of Ontario. The fear and prejudices I felt as a child have been replaced by a rich family history with strong Métis roots in the Georgian Bay Métis Community. I've learned that my grandfather, Louis Lamondin, is verified by the Métis Nation of Ontario in the Ontario Métis Root Ancestors Project. My grandfather is from the Solomon and Berger-Beaudoin family lines and, therefore, so am I. How wonderful it is today to celebrate what we've learned within a family who once felt only fear and shame about who we are.

As I pick over the bones of my life and try to make sense of it, I realize now that I made a dramatic change in direction at my dreaming-age of thirty-two. It was as though something unlocked, and I suddenly woke up. Reliving my lifetime on this Earth through the eyes of a septuagenarian is like creating the picture in a puzzle. Each small piece fits together and makes more sense with the others tucked in around it. I keep working away until an image finally emerges, held there by its parts.

So, why am I writing about all the cringe-worthy bits and pieces now? Because I have a lifetime of stories to tell, and I want to display them like a trophy while they're still bright and shiny enough to see.

Pat Lamondin Skene

PROLOGUE

The howling wind blows wild through my hair, as I stand like a forgotten ghost at the end of the pier. My scarf flies off my neck, making contortions in the air currents, before it collapses into the white caps. A frosty spray whips across my face and sends ghostly fingers reaching for the shoreline. I feel a blistering sorrow in the hollow of my bones.

The Bronte pier is deserted. I sink down to the wet cement, the cold dampness seeping through my jeans. Water has been at the core of my life for generations. Much of my Métis way of life as a young child was shaped by the river. How many times have I returned for comfort and connection to something bigger? But even the waters of Lake Ontario desert me these days. Dark thoughts stick to me like a shadow, creeping along with every step I take. I want to go with him. I just want to die to stop the pain. The clawing urge to follow him tugs at me like an undercurrent. Then I think of what that would do to my daughter and granddaughter, and my sobs threaten to crack me in half.

The swells come in harder, slamming against the side of the pier, retreating, and advancing, splashing over me, again and again. I lie there in the fetal position, soaking wet, an empty body drenched in sweat and cold water. That is, until a large black dock spider slithers up from the pylons and into my pant leg, jolting me back to life.

Wiping my nose on my sleeve, I struggle to my knees before standing up, like I learned in my yoga class for seniors. In squishy wet sneakers, I creep across the slippery dock to the waterside path. All I need now is a fall and another hip replacement.

I'm alone in our condo, sleeping in the bedroom where my husband spent his final days. His death was also the death of "us," after forty-two years of a shared life, and I struggle to sort through the rubble of my half of the memories. I'm just Pat with no Bob attached, and I don't know what that means. It's been four months and still, none of this seems real. I shower, change into dry clothes, and make a cup of Bengal Spice tea to warm up. It's May and the lake has a lingering coldness, even if the ice is long gone and signs of spring are poking through the gardens. I open the refrigerator, not because I'm hungry, but out of habit. The bare shelves stare back. The fridge hums along as it always has, as if nothing has changed.

But everything has changed. I'm alone for the first time in my life. What if I fall and no one finds me for days? What if I have a stroke like my mother or a heart attack like my dad? What if I get sick and can't take care of myself? I search the inside of my refrigerator for answers; it responds with a chilled silence. I retreat to my bedroom and wrap myself in his old grey sweater.

I've had to navigate many strong currents in my life and usually managed to struggle my way through. But now, at this late stage, I haven't a clue how to move forward. It's been a long upward hike for a shy little Métis kid from the sticks. So, how did I get to this point in my life and where do I go from here?

Part One (1949–1961)

You must do the thing you think you cannot do.

— Eleanor Roosevelt

CHAPTER 1

Tragedy and Resilience

I was four and a half years old when a chimney from an abandoned sawmill collapsed on my father and cut off his left hand. I remember how frightened I was the day it happened.

It was autumn of 1949, and my older brother, Bruce, and I had gone cranberry picking in a nearby bog after lunch. When we left, the kitchen was steamed up and filled with the rich smell of peaches. It was canning time, and Mom had dozens of jars lined up on the counter and large pots boiling on the stove. My younger sister Estelle sat at the table eating sliced peaches.

When we returned, excited with our bowls full and pants wet past the knee, a strange car was parked in the driveway. We burst into the kitchen anxious to show Mom our cranberries. There were two men I didn't know talking to her, and they all stopped to look up when Bruce and I came in. I could see Mom was crying. I'd never seen my mother cry, and I was frightened; I started to cry too, which made Estelle cry. One of the men put his arm around Mom's shoulders. She told us she had to go out for a while and Aunt Lily from next door would come to stay with us. Then she quickly left with the men. Although I didn't understand what was going on, that was my first memory of feeling vulnerable and afraid. Even as a young child, I could feel the security of my small world shifting.

As I got older and watched my dad struggle with adapting to a stump instead of a hand on his left arm, I wanted to know more of the details and asked my mom many times to tell me the story.

♦♦♦

We lived in Britt, Ontario, a small, unorganized township with a population of four hundred. The houses were built along the Magnetawan River off the shores of Georgian Bay. The name "Magnetawan" means "swiftly flowing waters" in the Ojibwe language. We lived on the fringes of several First Nations communities, including Henvey Inlet, Magnetawan, and Shawanaga. We called them Indian reservations back then. Britt is on the traditional territory of the Anishinaabe. My great-grandparents on my father's side moved to Britt in the 1800s from the Penetanguishene area. We are Métis descendants of the Solomon and Berger-Beaudoin family lines. With deep roots in the fur trade, my ancestors have lived in historic Métis communities since the 1700s, from Michilimackinac to Mackinac to Drummond Island to Penetanguishene.

Many Métis families like mine had travelled to the Britt/Byng Inlet area, where the logging industry generated jobs. The term "Métis" wasn't used in my community in those days, even though the word had been around for a long time, probably because no one admitted they were of Indigenous descent, and the language of our small community excluded any talk of such terms. Terms such as "French-breed" or "half-breed" were more commonly used. Although it was rarely discussed, I knew we were part French and part Ojibwe. Dad's family must have had a distinct story and generations of Indigenous heritage. Yet we were unaware of any of it and were brought up disconnected from the First Nations communities that were our neighbours. There was a deep shame and fear of being Indigenous due to anti-Indigenous racism, fear of losing work, and the negative impact on social standing.

Most of my aunts and uncles denied their heritage all their lives and resorted to racism against other Indigenous people to avoid rejection by society. We all based our opinions of the people who lived on reserves by the behaviours of those who blew into town in their pick-up trucks on Saturday nights and went to the Britt Hotel. Mom and Dad talked about the drunken brawls that usually broke out, and I was often wakened by their disruptive shouting and horns blasting as they drove past my house when the bar closed. My aunt Bernice would drive me to the reserve to show me how they lived. While some homes were neat and tidy and looked like most of the houses in Britt, my aunt would point out those that had broken-down vehicles in the yards, kitchen appliances on the porches, and unkempt properties. I was a child and knew nothing of the heartbreaking history of how Indigenous people ended up on reserves or any of the injustices that had occurred for decades. Nor did I know that not all Indigenous people lived on reserves. So, what I saw became my reality and the only thing I knew.

"This is not who we are," Aunt Bernice would say. "We are not Indians!" I'm sure my aunts had experienced prejudice all around them growing up. They must have also seen their share of Indigenous children being ripped from their families and forced into residential schools. Their fear drove out our ancestral stories, and the internal family prejudices became part of my life. I didn't want to be associated with "those people" either, and I was happy to further distance myself from them.

I had ash blond hair, green eyes, and a fair complexion, so I easily passed for white. My brother, Bruce, was also fair-skinned, but my beautiful sister Estelle was darker, with stronger Indigenous features. When she went to school, she was sometimes called "dirty squaw" by other kids in town. Some people threw dirty dishwater at her when she walked past. I remember one bully who threw her into a ditch and told her that's where she belonged. Estelle would come home crying, and it's sad to think Mom and Dad didn't react to these injustices. Dad stayed silent, and Mom would tell her to "rise above it," which was her recipe for most things to avoid confrontation and unpleasantness.

So, it was a surprise one Christmas when my sister and I received "Indian" dolls dressed in traditional buckskin clothing from my aunt Blanche, my mother's sister. We were not impressed. When spring came and the ice broke, we walked to the end of the dock and set them afloat in the Magnetawan River.

✦✦✦

While the little town of Britt was picturesque, it had a wilderness quality, with roaming black bears, wolves, venomous rattlesnakes, snapping turtles, and six-foot-long fox snakes that could catch you off guard both in water and on land. Like most Northern Ontario towns, Britt was notorious for the swarms of blood-sucking black flies, which appeared in spring, followed by a scourge of mosquitoes all summer. I took all this in my stride as part of my natural environment — along with the array of wildflowers, sweetgrass, beautiful waterways, fresh fish, bush berries, and locally grown farm vegetables. Britt wasn't big enough to have a town council or a mayor, so the local Jesuit priest, Father Ryan, ruled the day in this primarily Catholic town.

+++

Our little two-storey house was on the banks of the Magnetawan River; we could see the town of Byng Inlet across the water. We had a long dock with a boathouse that my dad built from old barn boards and railway ties. In summer months, we did cannonball jumps off the dock, fished for perch, built moss houses on the rocks, picked blueberries and raspberries, and climbed trees. In the fall, there were always cranberry bogs to visit and minty red wintergreens to find in the shade of the forest floor. I loved to search for jewelweeds, aptly named touch-me-nots. It always amazed me how the flowers would explode into the air with the slightest touch. In winter, we sledded down the hill beside our house, built snowmen in the yard, and skated on the frozen river.

We had no electricity, telephone, or indoor plumbing; two wood stoves heated our home. My dad wanted to switch to a coal-burning furnace and needed bricks to build a new chimney. The abandoned sawmill across the river in Byng Inlet had shut down a couple of decades before. And although many of the buildings were in a serious state of disrepair, my dad thought it was the perfect place to get enough free bricks for what he needed.

He set out with a crew of local men to dismantle the chimney from one of the remaining structures. But as the men chipped away at the mortar and loosened the bricks to load them into wheelbarrows, the building collapsed and pinned my father's arm under the rubble. The falling debris severed his left hand, leaving him bleeding and unconscious. A couple of the men carried him into the back seat of a car and rushed him to the Parry Sound hospital, which was about forty miles away on an old winding dirt road. My mom followed in another car, holding his severed hand wrapped in a towel on her lap. I can't even begin to imagine the horror she went through during that ride.

The doctors tried to reattach Dad's left hand, but in those days, small-town hospitals were ill-equipped for such miracles. I wonder now how he took the news. What frightening thoughts went through his mind when the reality of what happened struck him with full force? It hurts my heart to think about it.

+++

I remember bits and pieces of our life at home while my father was recovering. He spent about a month in the hospital, and it was difficult for my mom to keep in touch with the doctors. There was only one telephone in the middle of town in Buck Wood's house, where his sister Nelly managed the switchboard.

The first time the hospital called to speak to my mother, Nelly sent someone to our house to get her. It was about a ten-minute walk away. Mom was on her own with three small children, and she needed to get there quickly to take the call. So, rather than let us slow her down, she left us home alone on the sofa, side by side like sparrows on a branch, and promised us treats when she got home — if we didn't move while she was gone. We were all big tattletales, so we didn't dare even try to sneak off that couch. I remember shrinking away from the hot stove she always warned us about, just a few feet away.

My parents had never been gone from the house at the same time, and it felt weird being alone. While she ran to answer the phone in town, the three of us knelt on the couch and stared out the window, watching for Mom to return. I worried about what would happen to us if she didn't come home. As we watched for her to appear on the road, I played "I spy" with my brother to stop myself from crying. I remember the tremendous relief I felt when I saw her brown coat as she turned from the road to walk up the driveway. We all jumped up and down on the sofa and waved at her through the window.

We really didn't know what was going on with my dad, just that he was in the hospital. Mom looked sad all the time, and sometimes I heard her crying when she was alone in the kitchen at night. There was a heat grate in the floor of our bedroom over the kitchen. I could lie on the floor and see her through the grate. It hurt my stomach to watch her, but I didn't know what to do.

I think about my mother now and try to imagine how she felt. I can picture her rushing into town, sometimes in the snow, to take a phone call — all the while worrying about leaving us alone in a house with two hot wood stoves. Looking back, life sure was tough, but so was my mother.

She never canned peaches again.

+++

When my dad came home from the hospital, he had bandages on his arm, and he didn't smile very much. I felt shy around him, and sometimes I peeked into his bedroom. He always had his back to the door, and I didn't know if he was sleeping. So, I never asked him all the questions I had about his arm: how much did it hurt, did it bleed a lot, and why was there a scary-looking black leather hand on the dresser?

In the months that followed, Dad struggled with gangrene and went back to the hospital for additional surgeries and treatments. The doctors had to cut more off the stump several times before the infections stopped. How discouraged must he have been through all of that? How much pain did he endure? As a child, I wasn't aware of the extent of the challenges my parents were facing — they were well hidden. Mom kept things going in the family, and Dad continued to suffer in silence.

In later years, my mother told me the accident changed Dad's personality. She said he used to laugh a lot more and was confident and relaxed. I only knew he was still my dad — just quieter and sadder than he used to be. I remember my mom looked more serious when we sat down to eat supper. Sometimes, she left food on her plate, which I wasn't allowed to do without a good reason.

I look back on that now and think about the strength it took for Mom to stand by her man and take on so much responsibility for the family. And, without knowing it at the time, it taught me to persevere when things got tough. That subconscious grooming paved the way for some of the decisions I would make in my relationships later in life.

✦✦✦

My mom, Laura Charron, was born to a French-Canadian family in Sturgeon Falls. She was a beautiful woman with dark brown hair, huge brown eyes, and creamy white skin. Her parents, Delia and Olivier Charron, were cooks on a bush train that travelled to various lumberjack locations. At one point, they ran a large boarding house in Britt for workers from the Canadian Pacific Railway (CPR) coal docks. It was on one of those visits to see her parents that she met Dad. He lived in Britt with his family and had a job at the CPR.

Despite the mismatch in lifestyles, they were attracted to each other. Mom lived and worked sixty miles away in Sudbury and hated small-town life. She lived alone, played the violin, and loved her job at Silverman's Department Store, although she dreamed of becoming a lawyer someday. She enjoyed buying good furniture for her apartment and had the latest haircuts and fashions. Mom knew becoming a lawyer was beyond her financial abilities, but she still dreamed about it. Her ambitions went well beyond living in a small town. My dad, Bill Lamondin, disliked the city and had no desire to leave Britt, where his family had lived for well over a century. He and my mother dated part-time and went back and forth on the train to see each other for years, waiting for the other one to give in.

Eventually, when Mom was thirty-one and he was thirty-two, after dating for over a decade, I guess Dad wore her down, and she agreed to marry him and move to Britt. She must have loved him much more than she loved the city to leave her life there behind. Dad built a house on the Magnetawan River for them, and like many other Métis in the community who built houses along the water, my family were squatters on Crown land for many years. I have no idea what Mom thought of living in Britt before we kids were born. All I know for sure is that she never wanted our family to stay there forever and hoped one day we would all move to Sudbury. That wouldn't happen for many years to come.

✦✦✦

I loved going through the photo albums and always begged Mom to tell me about the stories behind each photo. My favourite pictures were those taken prior to Dad's accident during the years before they got married. They were always smiling, and she looked so pretty. She was still pretty as my mom, but not like the pictures with the fancy dresses and latest hairstyles and makeup. Dad looked dapper in those days, in his fedoras, white shirts, and dark suits. Mom and Dad looked like they were having fun … in the days when he had both hands. Now, she wore housedresses and no makeup, and Dad wore shirts with his sleeve pinned up over the stump on his arm.

My favourite "before the accident" picture of Dad was the one in his hockey gear as captain of the local team. I never got tired of asking her to tell me about the time he was in the middle of a game, and a spectator called him a "big cow on ice," and he lost it. He jumped over the sideboards of the outdoor rink and chased the guy all the way home on his skates before turning around. She'd shake her head and say Dad was a bit scrappy in those days — he never backed down from a fight. The father I knew would never do such a thing. At home, he was usually working alone in the yard or at the boathouse. And inside, he would sit quietly and listen to the radio, barely saying a word. He would always sit on the couch with his stump facing into the corner of the seat to hide it as much as he could from view. If there were more than a couple of visitors in the house or if things got too noisy, my dad would leave the room. I couldn't imagine him confronting or chasing anyone!

I think of him now, and I realize I never knew him as the man my mother met. Yes, he was still the kind, gentle human being she fell in love with. But it seems to me he was always trying to make himself invisible. How must he have felt seeing my mother carry so much of the burden? And did he feel guilt and remorse after convincing her to move to Britt to be with him, only to see her life filled with hardship? I don't know how she felt about these things; as a child, my parents were just my parents, and I didn't know enough to ask.

One day, when my brother and I were playing hide-and-seek, I found a large silver trophy tucked on a back shelf of the upstairs closet. It was black with tarnish, but I could see my dad's name on it. I brought it downstairs and asked my mom about it. She told me that Dad had won trophies for racing his two sled dogs on the ice, long before he and Mom were married. The huskies' names were Whiskey and Wine, which was ironic since Dad wasn't a drinker. Mom showed me pictures of her on the sled dressed in a white furry hat and jacket with matching white boots, ready for a ride on the frozen Magnetawan River. Mom looked beautiful, and Dad was dashing in his jaunty scarf and wide-brimmed fedora.

My mother told me the story about how a local man, who also raced sled dogs, was jealous of Dad winning the silver trophy, sponsored by the T. Eaton company. One night, someone sneaked onto the property and poisoned Whiskey and Wine. She said my father was sure it was the same man and confronted him, but he had no proof, and the man denied it. Dad never got over his anger about the incident and stopped racing. After hearing the story, I always felt sad when I looked at that blackened trophy in the closet — a reminder of how someone's jealousy had hurt my father.

✦✦✦

Bill Lamondin was a tall, good-looking Métis with the same green eyes he passed on to me. Dad had dark leathery skin reflective of his Indigenous heritage. Our ancestors can be traced back to the voyageurs and fur trade network in Ontario's northwest. But after generations of discrimination and shame, many families like mine had changed their

Métis surnames to further distance themselves from their Indigenous roots. My father told us that his family's original surname of Normandin was changed to Lamondin in the early 1900s to sound more French. Normandin is also listed on Dad's birth certificate. Regardless of the discrimination, he was still willing to serve his country but was not allowed to serve in World War II because of high blood pressure.

Although my father rarely spoke of our Indigenous heritage, I remember him saying that his father had relatives tied to the Ojibwe. His mother's birth name was Michaud, and my dad told us she had Ojibwe ancestors as well. He'd always look away when I asked him questions about it, and if my mom was there, the discussion was over. Mom was like my aunts, my father's sisters. She would swiftly put an end to the conversation if it veered in the direction of discussing who we were.

All I knew at the time was that I should not tell people I had a background that would associate me with the people living on the nearby reserves. As much as my conditioning was to reject any connection, I remained curious and always wanted to know more. I remember thinking that I loved my dad whether he was "Indian" or not. It was confusing for me to associate him with what I thought I knew. Sometimes, when I was with him in his boat, the *Seabird*, riding the whitecaps on Georgian Bay, he would tell me stories about how he and his father used to find artifacts, like grinding stones and spearheads, out on the islands. Dad had a grade six education and spoke English and Michif-French, his Métis language. As a child, I spoke some Michif (although I didn't know it at the time) but mostly Mom's Quebec French, which we called fancy French.

I realize now that many Michif and French words are similar. For example, eggs are called *li zef* in Michif and *les oeufs* in French. Bread is *pin* in Michif versus *pain* in French, and fish is *pwayson* in Michif and *poisson* in French. I crossed back and forth easily between the two languages until I started school when I was six years old and classes were all in English.

Dad was most at home on the water, and his Métis identity was shaped by his connection to Georgian Bay. Métis men made good lighthouse keepers because of their ability to navigate the waters and live in difficult situations. In 1883, my great-grandfather, Joseph Lamondin, became lighthouse keeper of the Gereaux Island Lighthouse on Georgian

Bay. There's an island across the channel from the lighthouse called Lamondin's Point, named after my ancestors.

Dad's father, uncle, and grandfather were keepers of the light for several decades. As a boy, Dad lived in the lighthouse with his parents and four siblings. My father often filled in for his dad during times of illness, so he knew the job well. But in later years, when he applied for the post, he was declined because of his disability.

When I was growing up, he often took me to the lighthouse. We would climb the narrow wooden stairs and stop on the second landing, where there was a small open space without a door. Dad explained this was where he had slept with his two brothers and two sisters. I asked him how they all fit into that tiny space, but he just laughed and said he didn't remember the room being so small when he was a kid. When we'd get to the lantern room at the top of the stairs, I loved to stand behind the rotating beacon that kept passing boats safe. It was magical up there, looking out on the blue-green waters of Georgian Bay, and the thought that my father once lived there added to my amazement.

The Gereaux Lighthouse is still there, although automated, so it no longer needs a keeper. Today, there's a Coast Guard station on the island next to the lighthouse. My father's love for the wilderness and the shores of Georgian Bay was deeply rooted in his upbringing and Métis heritage. And because my early life was steeped in that environment, it's deeply rooted in me as well. Like him, I have always held a strong connection to water for energy and renewal. Being near water is like coming home.

Other than our magical forays into the bay, Dad was distant most of the time and not actively involved in my life, the way most men are today with their kids. He had an even temperament and never said an unkind word. He ate meals with us and was always physically present with us as a family. But my dad wasn't much of a talker, and he liked to isolate himself from people. He never struck me as a happy man or an unhappy man, for that matter — just a shy gentle soul who needed solitude, someone who was maybe a bit broken around the edges.

CHAPTER 2

Wakes and New Arrivals

Storytelling is essential to our Métis culture, and my love for sharing stories started with my grandmother, Cecilia Lamondin, who I called Mémèr. She was my dad's mom; she married my grandfather at only thirteen years of age and moved into the Gereaux Lighthouse. Her new husband, Louis Lamondin, was twenty-nine. There was a rumour in my family that she married him to avoid the residential school system, but no one would talk about it. Mémèr's roots were hidden by the many name changes along the way.

My grandfather Lamondin died when I was very young, so Mémèr lived alone a couple of doors away from us. I visited her often, and we would crank up the Victrola and put on vinyl records to sing along to "Mockingbird Hill," "Teddy Bear's Picnic," and "You Are My Sunshine." I always looked forward to eating treats from a little wooden log house she kept filled with candy. I would lift the red roof and choose a peppermint or a humbug. But my favourite part of every visit was listening to her stories. She had a beautiful gold cut-glass canoe sitting on her window ledge. While I wrapped myself in her tales, I would stare at that canoe and watch the sun sparkle on the glass. I didn't know then that the canoe is the symbol of the Ontario Métis. Today, that little golden canoe has a place of honour in my home.

Sadly, I don't remember the details of many of Mémèr's stories. But there was one she told me when I was about nine years old that's hard to forget. She said when she got married she didn't know anything about sex or having babies. I didn't know much either at that point, but I knew enough to know that babies didn't grow in a Georgian Bay windswept pine. My friend had shown me a sketch of a baby in a woman's stomach from her mother's doctor book. I thought it was a horrifying picture, and both of us had no idea how the baby got in or out of there.

Mémèr said she used to spend her days swimming, fishing, and picking blueberries on Gereaux Island while my grandfather attended to his lighthouse chores. She told me that one day, she felt something move in her stomach. She was very upset and told my grandfather she had probably swallowed a pollywog while swimming, and it had grown into a frog. I'm not sure how my grandfather handled it, but the frog turned out to be her first child, Alcide. After that, she must have gotten the hang of it quickly because she had four more children in rapid succession. That story is a classic throughout our family and always gets a chuckle when someone brings it up.

I also remember Mémèr's story about why my dad had a raised red birthmark between his eyes. She said when she was pregnant with him, she was working in her garden, and one of the beets she was picking squirted on her forehead in exactly the same spot. She was convinced that was the cause of his birthmark. I know now that a freshly dug-up beet is not juicy and can't squirt on your face. But back then, I believed anything. Well, almost anything. Once she told my cousin and me that the secret ingredient in her macaroni salad was canned mosquito eyebrows. Helen and I went through her burlap bag of garbage looking for the empty tin, but we were sceptical when we never found it.

Whether her stories were real or imagined, I kept coming back for more. Sometimes, I went with my sister Estelle or my cousins Anne and Helen. Mémèr loved a good audience, and maybe it brought her joy to see how big our eyes would get, sitting on that green couch in her living room, eating humbugs and hanging on her every word.

+++

One Sunday, Bruce, Estelle, and I were walking to church with Mom, and I asked her why Dad never came with us. She said that since losing his arm, he didn't like being in public. Even as a child, I noticed that Dad often retreated to his bedroom to read his prayer book, and he never liked to join the weekend company. But my mom was her happiest when the house was full of people. I loved to sit on the stairs in the kitchen and watch her play euchre with my aunts and uncles. She was different on those occasions, more carefree and laughing with a joy I didn't see very often. I loved this side of my mother.

Dad was just always quietly there, cutting the grass, working on his boat, and shovelling fresh gravel on the driveway after a storm. When he could, he would stop work to come inside and listen to *The Happy Gang* on the battery-powered radio while he ate his lunch. Sometimes, he made us laugh by asking us to pull his finger. Dad kept to himself most of the time. So, we loved it when he was playful with us, which wasn't very often.

I always felt closest to him when we went out on the water in the *Seabird* together. I'd sit in the front seat with him quietly enjoying the sights and sounds of Georgian Bay while he skilfully manoeuvred his boat through the jagged rocks and dangerous shoals. We never wore life jackets back then; we all knew how to swim, and I felt safe when I was with him. We didn't talk much; we were silently connected in the moment by the water. Dad knew every windswept pine that greeted us and every treacherous rock that lurked beneath the choppy waves. He would even lift his stump up to rest on the edge of the boat, as opposed to tucking it in a corner of the couch as he did at home. This is the father I remember most, and I treasure those moments I had with him on Georgian Bay.

Before the accident, Dad had a job operating the trestles where the coal boats came in at the CPR docks in Britt. But he needed two hands to do the work, so the CPR fired him, leaving our family with no income. I asked Mom about that later in life, wanting to know how they managed. She told me she was relentless in her phone calls to the CPR and showed me letters she had written to their head office in Montreal, pleading for work on behalf of my father. Eventually, they gave him a job shovelling coal into the furnaces at the docks. They never offered him the option of doing anything else. It was a tough, sweaty job but the only one available to him, and I never heard him complain.

I think about him now, working in that windowless space and can imagine how cooped up he felt being confined to that dark room for eight hours a day.

I visited him often in that hot furnace room. In summertime, I'd go to see him in the afternoon after swimming and pick one of the wild roses along the roadway to put in my wet hair. After bouncing across the swinging bridge, I'd make my way along the tracks to the building where my dad worked. Sometimes, the big piles of coal in the CPR rail yard distracted me. I would climb to the top and slide down on my bum to the bottom as if I were on a toboggan run.

When I walked into the furnace room to see Dad, my clothes were often black with coal. He would smile and listen quietly while

I nattered on about little girl things. His face was always covered in coal dust too, and I remember how white his teeth looked when he smiled at me. Dad never had a lot to say, but he was always a good listener.

By that time, he was wearing a harness with a leather sleeve over the stump of his arm. It had a split-hook that snapped on the end, which he could open and close with his shoulder muscles. To use the shovel in the furnace room, he screwed a steel loop into the wooden handle. I used to watch him insert his hook into the ring and lift the coal shovel like he had two hands. In our shed at home, I sometimes helped to hold the tools for him while he attached similar loops into many of his own shovels and axes. On the rare occasion he got dressed up, he took the hook off and replaced it with a prosthetic — the black-gloved leather hand I'd seen on the dresser.

Some kids teased us about our "Captain Hook" father with the steel claw, but he never frightened us with it. Rather, he showed us how it worked, which took all the scary stuff away. We were close friends with some of our cousins next door. They were part of a big family. One day when my dad was working in the yard, I heard one of the older girls yell, "Look at the cripple!" She laughed, poking her sister and pointing at my father. I knew kids could be mean, but I felt bad for my dad. He simply put his shovel down and went into the house. So, I became a mean kid, too, and planned my attack.

The next day, when I saw her walking home from school, I shot back, "At least my father isn't Gooseneck Nye!"

Nye was the nickname for my dad's older brother Alcide. He and Aunt Lily were my godparents, and the parents of my nine cousins next door. Uncle Nye was a small man with an Adam's apple that bulged in his neck. He was a lovely, quiet person, who would never harm a fly. It was a mean thing for me to say, and my cousin started to cry and ran home while I kept shouting, "Gooseneck Nye! Gooseneck Nye!" I wanted to hurt her like she'd hurt my father.

By the time I sat down to supper that night, Aunt Lily had told Mom and Dad what I said, and my mother was not amused. Dad sat at the table with a funny smile on his face, so I thought I was okay because after all, Nye was his brother. But right after supper, Mom marched me next door to apologize to Aunt Lily, Uncle Nye, and the entire family. She said regardless of what anyone said about our family, I should always rise above the dirt instead of getting down and rolling around in it.

All eleven of them were sitting around the dinner table when we arrived at the back door. I blubbered through my apology to the whole family, but not just because I was sorry for what I'd done. Like many Métis households, Uncle Nye and the family had weekly toe-tapping singalongs in their large kitchen. They were a musical family with fiddles, guitars, harmonicas, a piano, and always someone playing the spoons. A few of us even did some jigging. I looked forward to singing with them in that kitchen on Sundays. I sure didn't want them to stay mad and stop me from going. Despite what I'd done, I liked my cousins and especially their family hootenannies. So, I wrenched out an emotional apology and continued to enjoy my musical afternoons.

+++

After Dad's accident, Mom continued to run the household while searching for ways to make extra money for the family. She started decorating wedding cakes, taking days to complete each one. I used to watch her for hours, as she worked with such patience to create a lacy dome made of icing for the little bride and groom on the top of the cake. She squeezed perfectly formed sugary rosettes around the edges of every layer and with a pair of tweezers added hundreds of tiny silver balls called dragées, which sparkled in the kitchen light.

But there were only so many weddings in a town of four hundred people, so she also began to sew. She took orders for everything from ordinary coats, dresses, and aprons to fancy long gowns for bridesmaids. If I sit quietly, I can still hear the whirring hum of the flywheel on her Singer sewing machine, coaxed on by the rhythm of her foot on the treadle.

+++

The Magnetawan River was an easy portal for fishers to access Georgian Bay. It was common for them to take the train to Britt and hire Métis guides like my dad to take them out to the fishing camps.

My father was known as one of the best fishing guides in town. Summer was always bustling with people looking for places to stay when the Britt Hotel was filled up. Mom convinced my dad to let her open a small tourist business called Edgewater Cabins. She had a good head for figures and worked out all the financial details. My aunt Lily had opened a similar business next door, and it was thriving. Mom and Dad purchased two old grounded houseboats, which they hauled up on our property, fixed up, and rented out. Once they had those up and running, they borrowed money from my dad's sister, Aunt Bernice, and added three more cabin rentals on our property.

Tourists filled both my mom's and Aunt Lily's cabins for the months of July and August, many of them repeat customers. They would book their dates a year ahead. Many hired Dad as a fishing guide during his summer vacations and weekends. Winter was a quiet time in Britt, so local stores and restaurants were happy to get the business while they could too. Mom had three small children to care for while she kept everything else going. The woman was unstoppable.

Then one day in the summer of 1952, something happened that did stop her in her tracks. Mom's sister, Blanche, and her husband, Fred, lived in a large house in Sudbury. My mother's mother, Grandmother Charron, had moved in with them after my grandfather died. It was the reasonable thing, Aunt Blanche and Mom decided, because my aunt and uncle had no children and led a much less complicated life than my mother. Aunt Blanche and Uncle Fred owned a small grocery store and barbershop, and Grandma Charron helped out in the store every day. That was several years ago, and as my grandmother aged and became frailer, she couldn't help out as she had been doing.

Aunt Blanche loved playing bingo almost as much as buying fancy hats. I can't remember ever seeing her without a "chapeau" as she called them. She had a hat on her head when she got up in the morning, she went up the stairs to bed at night still wearing her hat, and she ate all her meals with her hat on. I'm sure she took it off to sleep, but who knows? Maybe she didn't have any hair! She was a rather quirky aunt, giggled a lot, and would never divulge her age, not even to her husband, who just happened to be a few years younger. But she did win a lot at bingo and often secretly gave Mom her winnings to help us out, without Uncle Fred knowing.

I remember the day Aunt Blanche and Uncle Fred arrived unexpectedly at our door with Grandmother Charron and her trunk of clothes. I was upset to see my mom sobbing as she begged them to keep her, but Uncle Fred said they'd had her long enough. He could no longer stand living with her strange habits. I didn't understand what all the fuss was about, but I cried too because Mom was crying. I heard Uncle Fred tell Mom that she had become a "burden." When they left, I asked Mom what that meant, and she didn't answer me. She was sitting at the kitchen table with her head in her hands when they drove away and left my grandma in our living room.

But still, despite being overwhelmed, Mom took her in. She never held it against her sister, and they continued to visit as they always had. Aunt Blanche loved Mom, and I heard her say what happened was all Uncle Fred's fault and how sorry she was.

✦✦✦

Grandma Charron was in her eighties when she moved in and could speak only French. My family spoke French in those days, so we could communicate well with Grandma. We didn't have an extra bedroom, but Mom and Dad converted a small room off the living room for her. My mom had her sewing machine in there, and sometimes caskets were laid out in that room for the occasional family wake. There were no local funeral services, so many families like ours had open casket viewings in our homes for three nights before the burial service at the graveyard.

Before Grandma moved in, when I was about five years old, Dad's Uncle George died, and he was laid out in that room in our house. For three days, we looked at a dead body, and for three days, we smelled a dead body in that tiny little room. We were told to be very quiet in the house, especially when people came to see him.

One night when everyone was asleep, my brother, Bruce, dared me to go downstairs and touch the corpse's hands. He said I had to bring back proof I'd done it by taking the rosary Uncle George was holding. I'll never forget how creepy it was when I sneaked down the stairs through the darkness and slowly walked toward the coffin.

The lid was open, and I stood on the kneeling box to reach inside. I avoided looking at Uncle George's face in case he opened his eyes. With my heart pounding, I reached in and touched my uncle's cold waxy hands. I began to remove the black rosary beads wound around Uncle George's fingers. All I kept thinking was "What if he grabs them back from me?" and "Why is he so cold?" When I ran back upstairs with my evidence, Bruce told me it was a mortal sin. So, I ran back downstairs and threw the rosary into the open casket. I wasn't sad to see that room go when it became my grandmother's bedroom.

⁂

Grandma Charron was different from all other adults I knew. I used to sit on her bed and watch in fascination as she wet red crepe paper and blotted it on her cheeks to make rouge. She wore black laced-up boots and layered her dresses, wearing three or four at a time. I often helped her tie at least three aprons over her dresses. I'm not sure why she did this and never questioned it. We had a small house, so perhaps it was a lack of closet space, or she was just an oddball.

As Uncle Fred said, Grandma Charron had many annoying habits, and many of them really got to my dad. In the winter, when the pump didn't work, we kept pails of river water on our porch. When she wanted him to fetch some for the kitchen, she would simply sit in her rocker and sing out "Galoo, galoo, galoo" (a distortion of the French word for water — *l'eau*), over and over until Dad brought the water in. Or when she wanted him to bring up some potatoes from the burlap bag in the cellar, she would repeat "Potat! Potat! Potat!" in a high-pitched voice until she got her potatoes.

Grandma had white hair that she wound tightly around her head during the day. She layered several thick dark brown hairnets on her head like a woven cap to cover the white. Late one night when everyone was in bed, I went downstairs to get a drink of water and received a great shock. Grandma was walking through the kitchen back to her bedroom, wearing a long nightgown with her white hair brushed out and hanging below her waist. I'd never seen her without hairnets. She gave me a wave and a little toothless smile as I watched her go. She seemed to glide effortlessly across the floor — like a witch going back to her lair. Even though I knew she was my grandmother, this image of her terrified me, and it stopped my nighttime wanderings.

⁂

Grandfather Charron had spent his life working as a cook feeding lumberjacks in Northern Ontario while Grandma settled in Sudbury to raise my mom and her sister, Blanche. Once the girls were on their own, Grandma joined my grandfather to help out on the bush trains. I guess they'd learned to make meals from what they had available, and there was a strong French influence in what they made. My dad wasn't keen on her cooking, so Mom still made most of the meals. But I always loved eating Grandma's scrambled eggs with strawberry jam and a side of fried apples for breakfast. Although I didn't eat them myself until I got older, how could I ever forget the toasted orange and onion sandwiches she and my mother sometimes ate for lunch? Once in a while, my grandmother would make boudin, which I loved to eat with ketchup until I was older and found out it was French for blood sausage. I never ate it again.

Although she didn't talk much, Grandma Charron was always there for me with a big hug and a good French song. She let me rock in her big wooden rocking chair and sing while she peeled potatoes. She always washed the dishes and left the knives, forks, and spoons to the end. I would block my ears and sing louder while she made an awful racket, swishing the cutlery around in the metal basin with her hands like a human agitator. In spite of her many peculiarities, we kids just accepted her as she was. To this day, I think of my Grandma Charron when I see people with eccentricities that make them stand out from the crowd. It always puts a smile on my face, and I feel like cheering them on.

My grandmother was always happy in her own little universe, marching to her own rocking chair rhythm. She owned nothing fancy and just improvised with what she had. Grandma Charron wore her eccentricities like a comfortable cloak of indifference and joy. She taught me to look for the person behind the peculiar and appreciate the individual. She showed me that eccentric people are often just ordinary people who ignore the norms of society to express who they are in their own way.

CHAPTER 3

Gaslight Shadows

Bruce and I were often at odds with each other. I was no angel, had a bossy temperament, and was determined to get the better of him. Like the time I whacked him across the back with a straw broom that floated ashore, because I wanted the broom, and so did he. I knocked the wind out of him, and while I did feel some remorse, I got the broom.

As a kid, I was fascinated by fire. I regularly sneaked into my mom's box of wooden matches and usually had a couple in my pocket. We used to go down to the water's edge and pick tubes of dried reeds. We'd light the end and pretend to be smoking a cigar.

In the summer of 1950, when I was five and a half years old, I instigated a scheme that nearly burned down our house and the town. My brother, my cousin Wally, and I liked to go blueberry picking in the rocky woods behind our home. But the path we took was filled with juniper shrubs, which we called snake-bushes. They always scratched my bare legs when I walked through them. So, I suggested to my motley crew that we burn them down. The idiots agreed.

I was the only one with matches, so I lit the fire that day, and in an instant, the dry bushes burst into a fury, and we ran for our lives. I went screaming to tell my mother while the boys raced from door to door alerting the nearby houses. The locals formed a bucket brigade from the river to the bush, and people got ladders and dumped pails of water on their roofs in case the flames reached their homes. Eventually, they got the fire under control without too much damage, and of course Bruce and Wally told everyone that it was all my idea.

+++

In September of 1950, before my grandmother moved in and two years after my dad lost his hand, I was itching to start school. I walked around the house holding an old novel that belonged to my parents, pretending to read by making up the words and turning the pages.

I loved the papery smell of books and how they felt in my hand. I was determined to learn to read.

Britt Consolidated School was a local public school that housed students from grades one to eight. There was no kindergarten in those days, so if I went, I would start grade one. My mother wouldn't agree to let me go to school because she said I wasn't old enough; she repeatedly told me I had to be six. But I was five and a half, and my older brother, Bruce, was starting grade one. There was no way that I was going to be left behind with my little sister Estelle.

So, although my mother protested that I was too young to start school, I think she was also secretly hopeful I would get in and channel that disruptive energy I had into something more productive. Although our family spoke French, the local school taught English only. My mother was worried I wouldn't understand the teacher, but she'd already taught me my alphabet and how to count to twelve in both languages. I was ready to learn more. She finally relented, and I jumped up and down when she said she'd make me a new coat for my big day. A sewing genius and a magician with old dresses and overcoats, she always made us new clothes for special occasions. Out of instinct and necessity, she had become an expert at the creative recycling of old clothes.

With only a few days left before school started, I watched her work while I looked at the pictures in my Betty and Veronica comic books. She made my coat by taking apart an old brown overcoat of Dad's, washing all the pieces, and hanging them on the line to dry. When each section was carefully ironed out flat, she cut a smaller pattern from the best patches of cloth and skilfully sewed them together with the worn sides in.

She made me a lovely chocolate brown coat and added a checked collar and matching beret-style hat with material from the lining. Then she added some bright shiny buttons to make it look brand new. I felt like a princess when she tried it on me. I was all ready for my grade one debut.

On the big day, I got dressed early and couldn't eat breakfast, no matter how hard my mother coaxed. I pulled a chair up to the window and sat there in my new hat and coat, waiting for the school bus to arrive. When it stopped in front of our house, Bruce and I ran down the cinder driveway to climb aboard. The bus was actually a wooden boxy wagon drawn by a team of horses. The wagon was painted red and white and had a removable top and two long benches that carried about twenty students. The driver sat on the left of one of the benches to guide the horses.

A pulley system operated two small doors at the back, and the roof was so low we had to crouch to get inside. In the winter, the wheels were replaced with sleigh runners to glide across the snow. As far as I was concerned that first day, it was a golden carriage transporting me to a new adventure.

When we all piled out of the bus at Britt Consolidated School, I noticed there were two separate entrances. The younger kids were lined up at one door while the older kids were lined up at the other one. One of my older cousins was surprised to see me there and showed me where I had to go. My classroom had gas lanterns suspended from the ceiling as we did at home and a big cloakroom near the stove at the back of the class.

My grade one teacher was Miss Alice Pitts, and I liked her right away. She sat me in the front row and handed out lined notebooks, pencils, and the Dick and Jane books we would soon learn how to read. I felt so grown-up sitting at my desk. I loved using the pencil sharpener and breathing in the smell of chalk on the blackboard. I enjoyed everything about school.

Then it all came crashing down. Despite protestations from Miss Pitts, the school board said I was too young and kicked me out after only three days. Both my mother and teacher begged them to bend the rules. But rules were rules, and out I went like yesterday's lunch. It was such a heartbreaking way to end my first school experience, and I cried away my disappointment for days.

I spent many hours licking my wounds in my favourite spot on what we kids simply called the "big rock." It was a large rocky formation not far from my house that had been blasted to make room for the road many years before. There was a ledge cut out near the top in the shape of a bench. I loved to climb up and sit there daydreaming as I looked out on the water. It was a place I would return to many times during my childhood and, in later years, in my imagination.

✦✦✦

After my expulsion from school, life at home eventually got back to normal. I sang French-Canadian songs with my mother in the warmth of our small country kitchen. My favourites were "Au Clair de la Lune," "Ma Petite Vache," and "En Roulant Ma Boule." I can still see the soft glow of gas lanterns and evening shadows reflecting on the wall near the cook stove and smell the sweetness of apple bread pudding in the oven.

Suppertime was also storytelling time. We'd sit together at the kitchen table. Bruce, Estelle, and I would tell Mom and Dad stories about playing beanbag football, which one had held their nose the longest underwater, and hilarious tales of Mrs. Gendron's obnoxious goat. She lived in a tiny house next to the school, and her goat terrorized us at every opportunity. Dad would lean back in his chair and shake his head with a smile on his face while Mom listened and jumped up from her meal to get us extra helpings or to fill our glasses with more milk. It's a wonder the woman ever ate a hot meal.

A pump at the kitchen sink took water from the well. But it froze in cold weather. So in winter, Dad had to cut a hole in the ice and bring water up from the river. Even after he lost his hand, he continued to carry water by wearing a wooden yoke around his neck so that he could balance a pail suspended on each end. Life was tough by today's standards, but back then, it was just the way we lived.

I loved to sit in my grandmother's big wooden rocking chair in the kitchen and sing in the loudest voice I could muster. When my mother did laundry, I could hardly be heard over the gas-powered wringer washing machine that rattled and chugged its way through the morning. The louder I sang, the harder I rocked, swinging my feet back and forth to keep the chair in perpetual motion. Often, in my zeal to get the pitch just right, I got carried away and flipped over backwards.

Sometimes after supper, I'd corral Dad into the living room to turn on our radio for some toe-tapping country music, like *Don Messer's Jubilee*. I would often tie a flowered tablecloth around my waist and dance my jig for him, to the bubbling sounds of fiddles and accordions. Bruce mostly played with his fishing tackle and read Superman comics. Many evenings, Estelle and I were busy with our colouring books or clipping pictures from Simpson's and Eaton's catalogues to make our own paper-doll cut-outs.

I can still remember those gentle evenings of quiet chatter and a few giggles while Dad listened to the radio and Mom pored over the newspaper at the kitchen table as if she were studying for an exam.

Sometimes, she would take out a deck of cards and lay them out in a design on the table. When I asked her what game that was, she said she was reading cards and that she could see things that were happening by looking at them. I looked closer at the cards and asked her, "Can you see me in school?"

"Yes," she said. "I most definitely can." I took her word for it.

We took Mom's psychic ability for granted in our family. We didn't really discuss it; it was just something she always did. She was never showy about it and usually kept her readings to herself. She may have discussed her thoughts with other adults but not with her children. It wasn't until later in life that she would open up to me about what she was seeing in the cards.

It was a long wait, but the following September, I officially entered grade one, back in class with Miss Pitts. She was a kind, patient teacher who loved her students, and we loved her back. She would turn up decades later as a character in my first published children's book, *The Whoosh of Gadoosh*.

There were four classrooms in the school for grades 1 to 8, so each teacher taught two grades at a time. The extra year at home gave me a head start on learning to speak English, and with Bruce in school, we spoke more English at home. I was a quick study. Miss Pitts was the teacher for grades one and two and recognized I was ahead of my classmates, so she gave me work from both grades. She fought against the school rules and advocated to have me skip grade two and advance to grade three the following year.

A battle of teachers, school board rules, and opinions ensued, but Miss Pitts remained a strong champion for me to advance. In the end, the school grudgingly gave in, and I was admitted to grade three the following September, back in the same class with my brother. So, I guess I just needed to start over to get where I should have been all along.

CHAPTER 4

Lighting Up

Electricity was finally coming to our town. For months, I watched workers from the hydro company come in and out of our house with toolboxes, cables, and ladders. They put up new glass lights in the ceilings of every room, which would replace the gas lanterns and oil lamps. They built the bathroom we would have off our kitchen with new indoor facilities, a welcome change from the chamber pots and outdoor toilets we were using.

My parents dumped lime down the holes of the outhouses to reduce the stink, but I still always held my breath when I went in there. I was especially looking forward to having a real bathtub to replace the large, galvanized washtub we used on Saturday nights. It was the same tub Bruce and I used for plucking duck feathers when Dad went hunting. I remember the ripping sound the feathers made when Bruce and I pulled them out of the dead ducks. Then Dad would clean them all for Mom to cook.

One day, I was sitting high up on a branch in my favourite chokecherry tree in the front yard. My brother came by, saw me in the tree, climbed up, and grabbed the branch I was on. Then, he pulled it with him as he jumped to the ground and held it there. I was upside down clinging to the branch like a caterpillar, screaming for him to stop. Mom came to my rescue, and when Bruce saw her, he let the branch go like a slingshot, and I was thrown back up into the tree. Thankfully, I hung on and wasn't flung off into outer space. I taunted Bruce as he cleaned the outhouses for his punishment.

That evening, Mom told us we needed to stay away from the yard for the next few days. She said the hydro workers would be stringing wires from our house to the new poles outside. Mom said they had to cut down my special tree to clear the way. There were lots of trees in the yard, so I would find another tree, she said. But when I watched from the window as they chopped down my beautiful tree, I felt like crying.

I would miss climbing those branches and eating the sour chokecherries that puckered my cheeks and turned my front teeth brown. Mom put her arm around my shoulders, and I swallowed to stop the tears. She told me life was going to be different soon, and I should be excited for the changes to come.

But it was hard for me to know just how different things would be. I imagined that our town would have electric lights like the ones I'd seen in downtown Sudbury when I visited Aunt Blanche and Uncle Fred. I never forgot the flashing colours of neon lights that filled the darkness as we passed in the car.

The big day came on January 16, 1952. That morning, I jumped out of bed and ran down to breakfast with Bruce and Estelle. Mom was making fried apples with cinnamon. "You will always remember this day," she said, filling our plates. "Tonight, we'll have electricity in our house for the first time." It all sounded like pure magic to me.

The wait was unbearable, but eventually it was time to go. We all put on our rubber galoshes and winter parkas and left the house. Estelle and I were holding hands with Mom as we hurried toward the excitement. We could hear the bells of Holy Family Church calling everyone to the centre of town. Bruce and Wally ran past us, anxious to beat us there. Dad would miss the excitement because he was working at the CPR.

As we got closer, we could see people lined up along the street on both sides. Father Ryan was talking and laughing with some men on Buck Wood's porch. There was a banner stretched across the front of the building that read "Britt Welcomes Hydro." A group of kids came sliding into town on a sled hitched to a dog. Some women didn't wear winter hats, and I noticed they had taken the curlers out of their hair. They did that only for big events like the Britt summer bazaar, High Mass on Sunday, or Friday night dances with the Noelville Ramblers, a local family band from a nearby farm. Otherwise, they seemed to always have their hair wound in a swirl of pincurls or rolled up in those narrow aluminum curlers with the little red balls on the end.

I couldn't see much through the crowd, but I remember hearing a siren. Then a large green truck ground to a halt, and men in overalls climbed the tall wooden poles. Everyone cheered when a megaphone blasted with announcements I didn't understand. I moved closer to my mother and blocked my ears.

“Watch that light bulb hanging by the door at the side of the post office,” my mom leaned down to tell us. Just then, the light came on, and the crowd cheered even louder. Everyone clapped, including my sister and me, although at the time I remember thinking, “Is that it? No coloured lights like in Sudbury?” It seemed like an awful lot of fuss over a light bulb.

While the ceremony didn’t impress me much, I loved the feeling of excitement in the crowd and the smile on my mother’s face. The big show was over, and the crowd quickly dispersed, so we headed home. When we got back to the house, Dad was home and had the new kitchen light on. Bruce, Estelle, and I ran around the house and took turns flipping the switches on and off in all the rooms. The new bathroom wasn’t ready to use yet, but we had enough excitement without it.

We stayed up later than usual that night, and Mom and Dad had a hard time settling us down. I loved the grown-up feeling of being able to turn on a light in our bedroom without having them light an oil lamp for us. I felt much more excited about that than seeing the light come on outside the post office that afternoon. We jumped around upstairs and bounced on the beds, still pumped up from the day’s excitement. The kitchen was beneath our bedroom, and the ceiling shook when we got too rambunctious. Mom hollered up, “Settle down up there. Who wants chocolate milk?”

We all sat around the table eating a snack of peanut butter and corn syrup on toast, and stirring powdered chocolate Quik into our milk. Bruce leaned over to put some bread into our new electric flip toaster, when suddenly there was a crash on the floor right behind him. Our newly installed ceiling fixture in the kitchen crashed to the floor, narrowly missing my brother’s head. The bulb was still lit in the ceiling, and Mom said, “Don’t anyone move! There are chunks of glass all over the floor.”

We tried to suppress our giggles while Mom got a broom to sweep up. Dad said all our jumping upstairs had probably loosened the fixture. I guess the day didn’t end as expected, but it was a dramatic finale to a memorable moment in our lives nonetheless.

+++

More changes came one by one. First, we got a new refrigerator to replace our icebox, an electric stove, and a washing machine. Dad replaced our battery radio with one that plugged in, although I remember telling him that *Don Messer's Jubilee* sounded the same. I'm not sure what I was expecting. I enjoyed the luxury of our indoor toilet, which was finally working. Most of all, I loved taking long baths until the water turned cold.

In 1954, we got our first black and white television set and a big antenna on our roof. We got two stations if we were lucky. Every night, my brother would stand by the TV and shift the rabbit ears around until I told him I could see something move on the snowy screen. Sometimes, all we could see was the test pattern. But it was still exciting when we got to see *The Lone Ranger*, even if he seemed to be riding his horse Silver through a blizzard. It was new and exciting to have a television in our house, and we all sat down with Mom and Dad every Friday night to laugh and cry our way through episodes of *The Plouffe Family*. I still danced my jig for Dad once in a while after supper, but soon the room was too small for both me and *I Love Lucy*.

A year later, we got a telephone. The day it went in, I couldn't wait to call my friend Judy, who had gotten hers the week before. My finger kept slipping out of the holes when I dialled her number, and Mom had to do it for me. It was thrilling to talk on the phone, even though Judy lived only a few houses away. We had a party line, which was a shared phone line with other families. When I lifted the receiver, sometimes I could hear people's conversations — which I often did when my mom wasn't around.

Some things I took in stride then, but I think of now with horror. I remember when we moved from a gas washing machine in the kitchen to an electric wringer washer in the basement. The cellar, as we called it then, had a low ceiling and held a large storage bin of coal for our furnace. There was always a puddle of water on the floor around the washing machine after a rain. Estelle and I dreaded going down there to do the washing together. As we stood barefoot in the water to get the job done, we would squeal and jump from the occasional electric shock that would run up our legs. I wonder now why we weren't electrocuted.

✦✦✦

All of these changes eventually made our old way of life as obsolete as the lanterns that were stored in the shed. Through it all, Mom,

Dad, Bruce, Estelle, and I continued to gather around the kitchen table at suppertime and talk about our day. But our storytelling time was always cut short because a TV show was going to start.

One big event was getting running water. Bruce and my father no longer had to chop through the ice in winter and carry water up to the house, using shoulder yokes. After we got electric wiring and a telephone, the quiet softness of our evenings was replaced with the noisier lure of the television, which brought our family together in a different way. All these changes were exciting for me as a child. But looking back, I have often thought an intimacy was lost in the process.

+++

Mom loved all her new modern conveniences. But despite her amazing resilience in adapting to the many challenges she'd been through, she never warmed to living in a small town.

Some of Mom's women friends were transplants from the city, like her, and some were local women. While she was friendly with everyone, she didn't go out of her way to mingle or join any groups. As kids, we weren't allowed to have friends over, but we could have our cousins visit anytime. She taught us the meaning of kinship and caring for our own. Mom kept us focused on family and looking for something bigger than small-town living. But looking back from where I am now, I realize she never told us how to reach for a bigger future. Mom made sure we never considered ourselves Indigenous. But now I wonder how it was even possible to dream about who I could become if I didn't know who I was.

It hurts me to consider that my mom was prejudiced too. I wonder how her friends in Sudbury reacted when she told them she was marrying Dad and moving to Britt — a mixed-race community. Maybe it wasn't a good experience, and she didn't want that for us. I remember her telling me there was a man in Sudbury who had wanted to marry her, but she chose Dad. If my mother had her own secret regrets, I never knew. But her influences ran deep with me because I shunned small-town living my whole life.

Mom didn't like the winter months when our cabins were closed, and we didn't get visits from our many relatives who lived in Sudbury. She would stare out at the snow and the frozen river, saying, "There's not even a dog moving out there." Mom was happier in summer, except she was terrified of water and didn't know how to swim, so she rarely went in the boat with us. And she hated rainstorms, which could be fierce, with thunder and bolts of lightning rolling in from the open waters of Georgian Bay.

I can still see her running around the house sprinkling all of us with holy water as the storm approached. Then she'd crawl into the back of a closet to wait it out. I loved the rain and still do. If there was no lightning, my sister Estelle and I would beg Mom to let us sit on the lawn swing underneath my father's black oilskin fishing coat to stay dry. It smelled like the blue-green waters of Georgian Bay. We sang songs, happy in our cocoon while the rain pounded down all around us. I felt protected, as if nothing could hurt me when I was under that coat — the same way I felt when I was out in the *Seabird* with Dad.

+++

Something I find strange today but thought perfectly normal at the time was that we never had birthday parties, and neither did many of the kids in town. We never got a birthday gift, and I'm not even sure Mom made us a cake for our birthdays although I seem to remember biting on a nickel wrapped in waxed paper hidden in a slice of chocolate cake, so maybe she did. And while we always celebrated Christmas with a church service, lots of delicious food, savoury slices of warm French-Canadian tourtière, and a freshly decorated tree, it was never about the gifts. We always got a stocking filled with hard candy and fruit from Santa and one gift each, usually a doll for me and Estelle and a cowboy gun and holster for Bruce or a toy truck. I remember it as a magical time, and Christmas is still my favourite time of year.

Although we didn't have many friends at our house in winter, the summer months were filled with many cousins our age. We were always on the go, swimming, picking blueberries, playing beanbag football, and having sleepovers. Family was everything to Mom, and when our house was filled with aunts, uncles, and cousins, there was always lots of good food, euchre games, and belly laughs. Unlike my mother, Dad wasn't comfortable with a house full of relatives. He often left the group to sit alone out on the porch, or he went to bed. Our family all knew the accident had changed him and accepted him as he was.

I have no lifelong friends from childhood or my school days in Britt. But I've always had a special bond with my siblings. Of course, we had our share of clashes when we were kids. But as adults, we've never had a disagreement that caused division in our relationships. We've always been there to support each other unconditionally. A few cousins have been part of my life forever as well.

I often dream about our little house in Britt, reaching back to remember the simple comforts of that cozy amber kitchen. I think of Mom's delicious boulettes (meatball) stew, and holiday tourtières, and the smell of Dad's fried bannock — all traditional Métis recipes. When I think of my mother, I remember the gentle magician with warm brown eyes and lavender-scented dresses, singing French songs in the kitchen. When I think of my father, I think of a quietly thoughtful man who loved his family and worked hard to provide for us, despite his private struggles after losing his hand.

✦✦✦

One summer, Mom got the flu, and Aunt Bernice took her to see the doctor. But the flu ended up being a surprise pregnancy. She was forty-one years old at the time and thought those days were over. When she told us, we were all excited for a new baby. I hoped for a girl and wanted to call her Sally, like baby Sally in my Dick and Jane readers at school. Estelle wanted to call her Ruth because she had a friend by that name. My baby sister, Maureen Beverly Marie, was born in February 1954 when I was nine years old. Our house got very noisy with a crying baby, but we loved her a lot, even though her name wasn't Sally or Ruth.

Around the same time, Grandma Charron was getting weirder than ever and suffering hallucinations. She was also having a hard time walking and had a few scary falls. Father Ryan would sometimes come to the house to say Mass and give her communion in our living room. On one occasion, Grandma insisted she saw my mother sitting in a tree outside her bedroom window, kissing Father Ryan.

One day, Maureen was crying in her playpen while I was helping Mom change Grandma's soiled sheets. Suddenly, Mom just plopped on the bed and started to cry too. It scared me to see her like that, and I told her not to worry, that I'd finish the bed by myself. Shortly after that, she moved Grandma Charron to a nursing home in Sudbury. I remember my mom crying a lot around that time, but Dad seemed relieved when she left. My grandmother's strange habits annoyed him just as they had Uncle Fred.

I don't know how Mom did it all with a new baby in the mix. I didn't have many chores as a kid; we mostly spent our days playing outside. But Mom and Dad were always busy, especially in summer, when our cabins were usually booked solid.

Many tourists who stayed in the cabins came to Britt specifically for my dad to take them out fishing. I knew all the spots they would go to: Soffel's Hole, Duquesne Bay, and the Bustard Islands, stopping on one of the rocks for a shore lunch of fried fish and canned beans. I can still see the tourists coming up from our dock when they returned with long stringers of pickerel, large-mouthed bass, and muskie. It was odd that my dad was comfortable as a fishing guide when he avoided so many social situations. But out in Georgian Bay, he was at home, and fishing didn't require a lot of talking.

Despite everything Mom and Dad had been through, they were always gentle with each other but not publicly affectionate. I never saw them kiss, hug, or even hold hands in front of me, and they never raised their voices, openly argued, or fought when we kids were in the room. There were never any loud disagreements between them, and I have no idea if they privately battled it out when we weren't around. So, I was conditioned from a young age not to create conflict by arguing or raising my voice. Other than the odd squabble between the kids, temperaments were always on an even keel.

Mom and Dad were not demonstrative and never gave us big hugs and kisses either. Nor did they tell us they loved us that I can remember, but we had everything we needed. Mom was always there for us with clean clothes, a hot meal even at lunch, and for Estelle and me — a new hat from Simpson's catalogue for Easter church service. Dad worked hard and was quietly there when we needed him. They never passed on the financial stress they must have felt at keeping the family going, especially after Dad lost his hand. I felt well taken care of, protected, and happy, and I went to bed each night knowing how much I was loved.

All of these memories are guideposts for me even today. Have I romanticized them into something they weren't? Life was hard back then, so perhaps I have. But what I remember most are the feelings of belonging I had growing up in Britt along the Magnetawan River. And then, how those feelings were lost to me when I left. My memories of that little house warm me from the inside out, both in the days before and after electricity. They will always remind me of my roots and how fortunate I was to be a part of something so unforgettable.

Throughout my life, when I've faced difficult times, I still think back to those days growing up in Britt. I remember the peacefulness of sitting alone in my strawberry patch on a warm summer day, listening to the crickets chirping in the rocks, and tall grass around me. I take myself back to the ledge on the big rock near my house, where I often sat daydreaming, looking out at the river. When I close my eyes, I can feel the calm settling in from the memory. In my dreams, my little house is always encased in an amber glow, welcoming me back home. That little town of Britt and the swiftly flowing waters of the Magnetawan are still where I go for comfort and connection to who I am.

CHAPTER 5

Wimples and Guimpes

When the CPR engines made the transition from coal to oil in the mid 1950s, the Britt docks were closed, and my father was forced to find a job in Sudbury. With only one hand, he took what he could get, which was a janitor position at the Sudbury CPR station. He rented a basement room from Uncle Ernest and Aunt Muriel. My father had a lifetime of free family rail passage after his years with the CPR, so he came home to Britt every weekend on the train.

Aunt Muriel and Uncle Ernest had three children, Ricky, Anne, and Linda. Anne and I were close and spent many summers in Britt together. Anne was one grade ahead of me in school and attended Marymount College, a brand-new all-girls private school run by the Sisters of St. Joseph. It had just opened its doors in 1956.

In 1957, when I was twelve years old and ready for high school, my parents decided to send me to Marymount. I'd board with my aunt and uncle like my dad, who had been there for the past year. Despite their financial hardships, my parents scraped together the money for tuition and uniforms. I was afraid to leave my family and go to the city. My friends in Britt were all going to take a bus to attend Parry Sound High School. Mom reassured me that I wouldn't be alone. I'd be with my aunt and uncle's family, and my dad would be there too. She wanted a better education for me than what she thought the public high school could provide. But I still worried about being cut off from the only life I knew.

Mom convinced me to go, so the plan was set: Estelle and Maureen would continue going to the school in Britt and live with my mom, Bruce wanted to go to Parry Sound High School with his best friend, Wally, and Dad and I would live in Sudbury and come home weekends and summers. We would keep this arrangement until the whole family could move to Sudbury in a couple of years. Dad didn't want to leave, of course, but he knew it was necessary to get work. Mom wanted to eventually sell the house in Britt and buy in Sudbury, but Dad would never agree. He always planned to come back permanently when they were retired. Mom hoped Dad would change his mind in time, but he never did.

I was excited to share a room with Anne. We always got along and giggled about everything, driving Aunt Muriel crazy. I loved to sing with the family when Uncle Ernest played his guitar and Anne accompanied him on her accordion. I convinced myself that if I had to go away to school, this was a pretty good place to be.

So, in September 1957, I moved to Sudbury, all ready for my big-city adventure. At the time, Sudbury had a population of nearly 50 000, so it was a big change. I felt sad leaving my mom and siblings behind, but Dad was with me, and that made me feel better. Anne and I stayed up most of that first night, too excited to sleep.

The next morning, I laced up my new pair of black oxfords and slipped on a white blouse and grey-crested tunic in preparation for my first day in grade 9. My uniform was baggy on my skinny twelve-year-old body, and my clunky shoes felt like slabs of cement, but I thought I looked great. Although I felt a growing rabble of butterflies in the pit of my stomach, I was comforted by the fact that my cousins, Anne and Helen, would show me the ropes.

There I sat on my first day in my grade nine homeroom, proud of my new uniform and ready to begin my life as a high school city girl. My homeroom teacher was Sister Mary Stella, a tall, imposing woman dressed in a severe black and white habit, with a long wooden rosary that hung down the side of her robes. Her face was squished into a starched wimple that held her cheeks and chin in a vice-like grip. A large white guimpe draped around the front of her habit over her chest, like a giant bib.

After welcoming us to class and reciting a long litany of rules, she said, "I would like all of you to take turns and stand to tell the class your name and what your father does for a living." I thought it was nice that she wanted to know more about us as students. Looking back, I assume now she was trying to determine the hierarchy of who was who — perhaps prominent families and wealthy donors to the school. One by one, the girls got up, and I heard them say things like "My name is Lois, and my dad owns a chain of bakeries" "My name is Nicole, and my dad is the mayor" "My name is Polly, and my dad runs a construction company."

There were many daughters of doctors, lawyers, and other middle-class families. I found it interesting to hear what the girls had to say, and when it came to my turn, I stood up and announced, "My name is Patsy, and I'm from Britt. My dad is the janitor at the CPR station downtown." Some of the students sniggered and looked at each other. I remember feeling the sudden heat in my face and being confused about what I'd said or done wrong.

Sudbury was a mining town, so a few of the girls' fathers worked in the Inco and Falconbridge mines. But that seemed a more acceptable profession than the one my dad was in. I don't remember any other reaction from my class, but the imprint of that moment stayed with me. It marked the moment when I felt different from my classmates.

Many of the girls were rich, privileged, and cliquey. Others, like my cousins Anne and Helen, were none of those things. But unlike me, they were from Sudbury and found it easy to find their place with a group of friends. Once the nuns and my classmates knew the area I was from, did they treat me differently because that identified me as an "Indian" or "half-breed"? Or was I just socially unacceptable because of what my dad did for a living? While I think announcing where my father worked had an impact on how they saw me, I didn't belong in their life of privilege. Many girls had known each other through grade school, and they were familiar and easy with each other.

There were a couple of other classmates in the same outcast boat as me, a Syrian girl and a student with really bad acne. But I couldn't seem to step out of my awkwardness to make friends. I didn't get picked for teams in gym class, I wasn't invited to any of their homes, and I was never included in their lunch groups. Anne and Helen made things easier for me where they could, though, and thankfully asked me to join them at their grade 10 lunch table.

This was my first experience with class distinction and the feeling that I wasn't good enough, as if I didn't belong. I was disconnected from my family and community in Britt, and that disconnect left me feeling adrift in a strange world. I felt alone and afraid, and I shrank deeper into myself with each passing day. I clung to my cousins as much as I could and lost interest in studying or getting good marks. The nuns frightened me, many of my classmates laughed at jokes I didn't understand, and my oxfords hurt my feet. I was a long way from the eager little spitfire who skipped grade two with Miss Pitts. I endured the days and hated school.

At home, there were many good times with Anne and her family. I loved listening to her practise "Over the Waves" on the accordion, even though it always put me to sleep. After supper, we did the dishes and giggled while we harmonized to "Bye Bye Love" and "Wake Up Little Susie." At least, life at home with Anne was fun.

But school was a different story. The principal at Marymount was Sister Estelle, a tall, stoic, unsmiling woman, nothing like my own sister Estelle. But she was gentler than some of the other nuns, who were often mean-spirited and cruel, constantly patrolling the halls looking for trouble. The nuns were very strict about wearing makeup and bouffant hairstyles. Once when I went to school with my hair backcombed and piled high into a beehive, Sister Mary Stella marched me off to the bathroom to wash it out.

Sister Alicia was the worst. She was about four feet eight in all directions. She was always eating something and had the habit of hiding food in the classroom. And what a holy terror she was! She screamed at me in the hall once because the hem of my tunic wasn't exactly fourteen inches from the floor. She actually kept a measuring tape in the pocket of her habit for that purpose. I often forgot to wear my blue ribbon tie, and she would pull me out of line with other girls who weren't wearing theirs and lecture us on the importance of honouring the sanctity of our uniform.

"It's a sacred symbol of the school," she would say. "You're being disrespectful!"

She was also my algebra teacher, and I was nervous in her class. It was hard to concentrate on her lessons while wondering who she would yell at next. She made me feel small and worthless.

On one occasion, the nuns had agreed to a volleyball game between our students and the boys at St. Charles College. We were all excited for the big day because this had never been allowed before. On the afternoon of the game, we gathered at the windows as the boys approached the school. All the nuns had agreed to the match, including Sister Alicia. But when Sister Alicia saw them coming up the hill, she screamed, "Lock the doors, lock the doors!" And just like that, the doors were barred, the game was cancelled, and we were protected from the male invasion. The boys, true to their natures, called Marymount "Cherry Hill."

Our gym uniform was a royal blue one-piece dress with attached bloomers and an overskirt. We had individual locked cubicles where we changed from one uniform to the other, never to be seen naked by other girls. For our showers, we went into our cubicles, changed into a terry robe and slippers, and went into our individual showers with locked doors. Half of our gym time was getting dressed and undressed into different garb to hide our bodies. At the time, I thought this was perfectly normal because it was all I knew. We were very modest growing up, and I'd never seen my brother or sister naked at home. Even Anne and I didn't dress and undress in front of each other.

Once a year, we had religious retreats at the school, where we had to abstain from talking at home and at school for five days. It was my favourite week of school because there were no classes and the nuns participated as well, so they couldn't yell at us. The silence was lovely. It was a full five days of Mass services, prayers, guest speakers, and a lot of propaganda on recruiting us for the nunnery. During the retreat in my final year, we had one speaker I'll never forget. He was a young, energetic priest, who had us all enthralled with his unconventional lectures and good looks.

One morning, in front of a packed gymnasium, he talked to us about sexuality. He had our complete attention when he described how some girls fainted during what he called "the raptures of lovemaking." There was a collective gasp from the nuns in the gallery, followed by a major rustling of wooden rosaries and a clatter of leather nun-shoes on the terrazzo tile. They rushed to the stage, and he was quickly ushered away. We never saw him again.

+++

One Friday after school, we were packing up in the locker room, and a group of girls were complaining about a test we were getting on Monday morning. We had to memorize the long soliloquy from *Macbeth*: "Is this a dagger which I see before me."

"Stuff it!" I heard one of them say. "Only an idiot would memorize Shakespeare."

I got the nerve up to say, "But you'll fail if you don't do it."

"Not if you cheat," she whispered, and they all giggled. "We all do. You wanna try it?"

I felt the heat in my face and nodded. She explained how I should write out the passage on a small piece of paper and fold it into the sleeve of my blouse. Then, all I had to do was copy the words during the test. It felt good to have a secret with this popular group of girls. So, I joined the cheaters club and enjoyed my weekend without homework.

On Monday morning, my heart was pounding when the test was ready to start. Sister Mary Stella sat quietly at her desk at the front of the class. It was all working well. I was sneaking peeks at my note and writing out the passage. Suddenly, she got up and walked down the aisle, stopped at my desk, and reached into my sleeve! Why would she catch me and nobody else in the class? She hauled me to the front of the room and gave me a berating for my heinous act. The rest of the girls watched in silence as my humiliation grew with each word. They had shared one of their popular-girl secrets with me, and I blew it while they all got away with it. I was devastated for days about what I'd done. Then I wondered if the other girls set me up to crash and burn. Did someone tip off the teacher, or was I just terrible at cheating?

I eventually approached Sister Mary Stella, who was standing outside her classroom. I apologized for my behaviour and sobbed uncontrollably into the starched white guimpe of her habit. She simply said, "Why can't you be more like your cousin Anne? She's a very good student and nothing like you." And with that hurtful bit of advice, she walked away from me, and I cried even harder.

I felt humiliated, alone, and more than anything, I wanted to go home to my mother. I wanted to make her understand I didn't belong at Marymount. But I knew going home wasn't an option my mom would talk about. She saw Marymount as an elevated level of education for me. I didn't tell Dad how I was feeling because he worked odd shifts, and we never had much privacy with seven of us living in my aunt and uncle's small bungalow.

✦✦✦

By grade eleven, I'd had enough of Marymount and decided to make a bold move. I wanted to transfer to the local high school for my final year. When I gave my notice in June, the principal, Sister Estelle, called me into her office. She said she was very disappointed in me for wanting to leave, and if I transferred out, she would have to fail me. That meant I'd have to repeat my grade eleven year at the new school.

I was confused because I'd already gotten my marks.

"Those are your marks if you stay at Marymount," she said. "But if you transfer out, you will have some failing marks in the transcripts to the new school." She paused and leaned forward on her desk. "But if you stay, you can continue on to grade twelve here."

I looked at her unsmiling face squished in her wimple, her eyes watching me without blinking. I felt trapped with nowhere to escape.

"Okay, I'll stay, Sister," I told her, and in that moment, all my excitement about escaping to a new place drained away. When I told my parents what happened, Mom said, "I'm sure Sister Estelle knows what she's doing." In those days, our parents were programmed not to question people in authority, especially people of the Church.

I later found out the same thing happened to my cousin Helen. Despite her excellent grades, they threatened to fail her when she told them she was leaving after grade eleven. She was bolder and braver than I was and left anyway. The school followed through on their threat, and she repeated grade eleven at the new school. She just wanted out.

In my final year at Marymount, I counted the days for school to be over. I already had a job offer with Bell Telephone and would be starting in July. I knew I was leaving and couldn't be bothered to study for my exams. But there were consequences. I felt sick when I saw my mom's face as she read my report card. I'd failed history with a forty-five percent mark, which meant I couldn't graduate from grade 12, something I have always deeply regretted and never told anyone. While my parents knew, I never discussed it with my siblings, my husband, my daughter, or my granddaughter — until now. I have been so deeply ashamed of not graduating from high school. Strangely, it's the one secret regret I carried all my life, unable to forgive myself for what I did. I thought people would think less of me, as I did myself, even though I went on to achieve other accomplishments.

✦✦✦

My Marymount College days are long gone. And while those years were not enjoyable for me, I realize now that I was ill-equipped to handle such a change in environment. Yes, the nuns could have been much more helpful, but my experience also had a lot to do with who I was at the time — lacking any confidence to step into my new situation. I was younger and less worldly than the rest of the girls in my class, as well as being painfully shy, socially awkward, and intimidated by my more confident classmates.

I was put into a situation with all good intentions. My mom wanted a better life for me and thought a private school in the city would do the trick. Miss Pitts had fought to move me ahead of my class, forever leaving me the youngest student among my peers. I always felt lost and terribly lonely for my family, despite the kindness of my aunt and uncle.

The experiences of many other students I knew, including my cousin Anne, were very different. Anne had attended a Catholic elementary school with nuns and was used to having them as teachers. She always got good grades, was involved with sports and music lessons, and had a job after school at the hospital. I had none of those extracurricular activities. I accept that my unhappiness was much of my own making. However, I simply didn't have the life skills necessary to acclimate to a foreign and sometimes hostile environment.

Did I learn anything else while I was at Marymount? I never cheated again in my life, so there's that. And Sister Mary Stella constantly preached about our looks. She would repeat over and over, "Your hair is your crowning glory, girls." Well, I've always had nice hair, so I guess I can thank her for that too.

Although not her intention, what Sister Mary Stella did by asking us the question about our father's occupations taught me to treat everyone with respect. Throughout my life, I have tried to be especially kind to those who struggle daily to make ends meet. It's too easy to become invisible in a society where status and social standing mean so much to so many. I walked away from high school more careful about disclosing too much information about myself. I began to understand why my family kept a tightly woven circle of relatives. There was comfort and belonging in a group.

CHAPTER 6

A Fork in the Road

I hold no nostalgia for my Marymount College days, and my relationship with the Roman Catholic Church was forever altered. I found it hard to separate my experience with the nuns from my faith in a religion I'd been brought up to honour and respect. I still held on to my own sense of spirituality, but eventually stopped attending Sunday Mass.

I was happy to leap out of my black oxfords and anxious to start my working life as a long-distance telephone operator. I was sixteen years old, and all I wanted was escape and freedom. Then, one week before I was to start work at Bell Telephone, I got an unexpected proposition.

Mr. Henry Powell was a very wealthy businessman who came into my family's life when I was only four years old. We met in a restaurant in Parry Sound when Dad's sister, Aunt Bernice, had driven Mom and me there in her fancy new Packard. Aunt Bernice was married to Uncle Art, who was captain of an oil tanker on Lake Michigan. They lived in Munster, Indiana, but my aunt spent summers in Canada. Aunt Bernice was an attractive woman, who loved to wear her blouses tied above her waist, stylish shorts, and wedge heels that showed off her long, slender legs. She was an incorrigible flirt.

I remember some details of the day we met Mr. Powell, and Mom filled in the blanks as I got older. She said we were eating lunch at a diner in Parry Sound when a stocky man in a dark suit approached the three of us and introduced himself as Henry Powell. I know now that he would have been about fifty years old at the time. He said he had no children of his own, and he complimented me on my blue crocheted dress and long braids. My memories are hazy, but I remember looking at the thin black moustache that stretched across his top lip when he smiled at me, and I remember the light blue dress I was wearing.

Mom said they talked for a while, and he told them he lived in Toronto but had a yacht moored on the southern end of Georgian Bay in

Midland. He told Mom I was a remarkable-looking child and asked her if he could visit us in Britt on his boat. As weird as that all sounds to me now as a parent, she agreed. My mother was a bit sceptical about the whole thing and told me years later that she was convinced he was after Aunt Bernice. But we would find out it was me he was interested in, not my aunt. That day started a strange relationship between us that would continue into my adulthood.

Every summer, Mr. Powell anchored his yacht out in Georgian Bay, and my dad took the outboard to pick him up and bring him back to our house for a few hours. On those visits, he sometimes brought me small gifts, like chocolates and colouring books. Once he gave me a field guidebook about birds of North America. I thought it was a stupid gift because I saw lots of birds every day in Britt. But when Mom sat with me to look at the pictures and read the descriptions, I realized there was a lot I didn't know about birds. I ended up loving that book.

There was one gift Mr. Powell gave me that stands out from the rest. He arrived in Britt one day in a black chauffeured limousine instead of his yacht. I watched through the window as the enormous vehicle pulled up in our driveway. I couldn't see who was inside because the windows were too dark. I'd never seen such a huge car. A couple of townspeople were passing on the road and stopped to watch it park near our house.

Mr. Powell got out of the back seat. The driver opened the trunk and passed him a large box tied with a pink ribbon. I ran to the back door with Mom, and she invited him inside. He put the box on the kitchen table and sat down. I stood beside his chair, as he held my hand and smiled. "This is for you," he said.

Inside the box was a soft rubber baby doll along with a complete wardrobe of doll clothes — terry sleepers, knitted sweaters, hats, booties, and cozy blankets, as well as baby bottles, diapers, and a tiny soother. I tried hard not to cry. I threw my arms around his neck and kissed him on the cheek. It was the first time I'd shown him any affection, and his skin felt scratchy, like the asphalt shingle siding on our house.

Mr. Powell explained to my mother that a good friend of his had lost her child at birth. In an effort to heal from the tragedy, the woman had lovingly created this layette of homemade clothes for a baby doll and asked him to find a home for it. I listened to him telling her this story, not fully understanding until I was a bit older. I treasured his gift for years and used the large box as a crib in my room.

Often, I would go on his yacht with Aunt Bernice for day excursions in Georgian Bay. Sometimes, Bruce would come too. And while Mr. Powell ignored my brother and was polite to Aunt Bernice, who always fawned over him, I got all his attention. Looking back, whether by design or not, I see that I was never left alone with him. In today's world, there would have been red flags and suspicions about the time he spent with me. But I didn't sense anything creepy about Mr. Powell, although I didn't like sitting on his knee or the feel of his prickly moustache when he kissed my cheek. He always had a surprise up his sleeve to entertain me, with a magic trick or a hidden treat to find on the yacht. He often talked to me about what I wanted to be when I grew up, and my answer was always the same. I would tell him that I wanted to be a teacher like Miss Pitts, my grade one teacher, and that I thought it was the best job in the world.

I don't know for sure if Mr. Powell ever helped my parents out financially. After my dad lost his arm and his job at the CPR, Mr. Powell offered him the opportunity to run a general store in a Northern Ontario town where Mr. Powell owned a lumber mill. While my mom was receptive to the idea, Dad declined. Running a store would mean too much social contact for him, and he didn't want to move away from Britt.

✦✦✦

When I was between the ages of eight and fifteen or so, Mr. Powell called my father several times and asked him to bring me for a visit to his home in Toronto. My dad and I would travel there by train and stay with Kay and Cecil Lacroix, who came to Britt almost every weekend to stay in our cabins and go fishing. They lived on Dundas Street downtown near the Brown Derby, and Mr. Powell would send his big, black chauffeured car to pick up Dad and me. Sometimes, my brother, Bruce, came on the train to Toronto with us, but he was never invited to join us for the visit. Looking back, I find his exclusion of my brother rude and his focus on me strangely inappropriate. But I was with my dad, and I thought nothing of it at the time. I felt special to be the centre of attention and was impressed by the big car that came for us. My sister and brother didn't seem to mind that all his attention was on me, and I just took it for granted. Looking back, I'm sure my father and mother felt intimidated and were somewhat awed by Mr. Powell's money. He lived such a different life from us, and my parents seemed impressed by the attention he showered on me.

Mr. Powell had a large home in the wealthy area of Rosedale in Toronto. I'd never seen a place like it. Climbing vines covered the stone exterior right up to the roof. I remember his house being full of beautiful surprises. On one visit, he asked me to sit on a green and white striped chair in the sunroom. As soon as I sat down, music blasted from the speakers installed under my seat. He and Dad laughed when I jumped off and crawled under the chair to check it out. He was like a kid showing me a new toy.

Mr. Powell offered us drinks and something to eat. Then he took my hand to show me around the main floor of the house while my dad followed behind. He asked me if I had ever seen a house like his, and I told him I had not. I was about ten years old at the time. He asked me to sit on his knee again, and I said I wanted to sit in the music chair instead. So, he sat in the music chair, and I sat on his knee. I remember looking around the room, and he smiled a lot at me and told my dad what a special little girl I was. It made me feel happy to hear that. Dad was always quietly in the room, and he and Mr. Powell sometimes talked about fishing and the challenges of manoeuvring his yacht through the treacherous shoals of Georgian Bay. Dad always looked uncomfortable and anxious to leave.

Another time, he took my hand and led Dad and me upstairs to a locked room that held a massive collection of antique clocks and watches. The walls were covered with a variety of fancy ticking clocks, and a few glass-topped display tables held dozens of vintage pocket watches and other timepieces. I told him I liked the sound all those clocks made, and he said it was like having a room full of beating hearts. I loved that image and always asked to see his clock collection when I visited him.

Once when Dad and I got there, Mr. Powell took us upstairs to the clock room, where he took out a large, ornately carved wooden chest from the closet. He opened the box to show us a set of gleaming gold dinnerware that had belonged to one of the King Georges. He said he purchased it on a trip to England. When he let me hold one of the heavy gold plates, I asked if he used them to have his supper. He laughed really loud at that and said no he didn't, but it was a good idea. Then, he turned to my dad and jokingly said, "Hey, Bill, these would make great dishes for a shore lunch out in the bay."

Dad didn't talk a lot when we were in Mr. Powell's home, and he always seemed to have a reason that we couldn't stay long. Once on the way home, he was very quiet and told me he just didn't understand why people spent money on such useless things. He shook his head and said Mr. Powell had so much, what more could he want? I've thought about that statement over the years and wondered if my dad was referring to more than Mr. Powell's money and possessions. Did he think the man saw me as a little white girl who needed to be rescued from a poor Indigenous family? Was my dad worried Mr. Powell would take me away into his rich white world?

When I was about fourteen, Mr. Powell took a round-the-world cruise that lasted for months. Before going, he gave me his travel plans, complete with a list of ports and addresses where the ship would be stopping during the trip. He made me promise to have a letter waiting for him at each port circled on the itinerary. Looking back, I'm not sure how the timing on all that worked, but I did what he said and mailed off my letters. He sent me beautiful postcards and gifts from faraway places, which opened my eyes and made me curious about a world I didn't know existed.

I would stare at the postcard pictures and daydream about what it would be like to be in countries so far away from Britt. I thought China was more beautiful than all the others, and I treasured the delicately beaded blue sweater he sent me from there. I would sit on my swing and close my eyes, pretending to be in places with names like Singapore, Greece, and Bombay. We had no library in Britt, so all I had were the words and pictures on his postcards. In my adult years, I was the only one in my family who developed a thirst for travel, and I often wondered if this experience planted the seed. Decades later, I would buy another beaded sweater when I took a trip to China.

✦✦✦

So, when Mr. Powell made the proposal to my parents and wanted me to go live with him in Toronto, it's not like he was a complete stranger. He said he knew it was my dream to become a teacher, and he would like to help by paying all expenses for me to go to teacher's college. He told us he could get a tutor over the summer to help me pass history, so I could graduate and be ready for September.

After he left, Mom and Dad talked to me about it and told me it was up to me to decide what I wanted to do. In today's world, that punt to me at such a young age by my parents seems terrifyingly wrong in so many ways. But looking back, it was a different time, and I'm sure they were in awe of his wealth and thought only of what he could do for my future. I believe they were both very naïve when it came to behaviours outside of their experience and would not have even considered that Mr. Powell might have dishonourable intentions. They had known him for years by that time and trusted he was trying to help me grow beyond the boundaries of a small town. Dad didn't know what to say to me because he couldn't even imagine making a life in a large city. And although my mother never once pressured me, she told me it was a dream come true and saw it as a huge opportunity. She always wanted me out of Britt and into a bigger life, a life she missed out on. But I still sensed her trepidation about my accepting his offer, when she always added that Toronto was so big and so far away.

Up to that point, my main focus in leaving Marymount was to escape the confines of a convent-like environment and find some freedom working for a living. It never occurred to me to become a teacher because my parents couldn't afford to send me to college. I'd given up that dream long ago. Now, right in front of me was not only an escape route but also an open door to fulfill a dream I thought was lost.

I liked Mr. Powell well enough, even though he was different from my family. But something felt wrong. He'd been married all the years I'd known him, yet I'd never met his wife, Edith. She was always absent during our yacht visits or away when we went to their home in Toronto. Mr. Powell never mentioned her, other than to offer excuses for her absences. Perhaps she didn't approve of his attention to me. I didn't have the maturity to think all this through, but it was something that I found unsettling. If his wife had been friendly to me over the years, it would have been easier to accept the offer and see it as an opportunity. I talked to my mom about it. She said Edith probably didn't approve of his attentions to me and our family, that she looked down on us as country bumpkins, beneath her high-society lifestyle in Toronto.

I thought about accepting his offer and simply staying out of his wife's way. Or maybe she would grow to like me in time. Then I wondered if she even knew he was planning all this. Surely she would want to meet with me before I moved in. Looking back, I wish I'd been confident enough to ask him outright about Edith.

Although I couldn't shake my strong feelings of unease, it was an alluring opportunity that made me feel special. Here was this important man offering me a future I didn't know I could have. However, as much as I was looking forward to enjoying my freedom outside the confines of the convent school, I wondered how this would be any different. I thought about how much I would be tied to him for everything. Toronto was so far from home. How alone would I feel living in that big house with two strangers? Britt had only one main street, so how would I ever find my way in a city that big? That didn't sound like freedom to me; it was just too scary to even think about. My decision wasn't hard to make.

I turned him down as nicely as I could and quickly put all thoughts of his offer behind me. I got ready to start my new job as a telephone operator. I don't think Mr. Powell pushed it any further with my parents, and we continued to maintain contact.

⬩⬩⬩

When I was about eighteen, I visited Mr. Powell in Toronto with a boy I was dating. The visit did not go well. Mr. Powell was rude and condescending and left my friend standing in the foyer while we went upstairs to the clock room. When I came back, I quickly made excuses to leave. I felt embarrassed for putting my friend through that, and I never went back to the house again.

His contacts became less frequent as I got older, and he was often drunk when he telephoned. When I was twenty-one, I called to tell him I was getting married. He was quiet for a moment and then asked me if I loved the man. He grilled my future husband on the phone and told him to treat me well. He didn't come to the wedding, but he sent us a set of French provincial nesting tables as a gift. After I was married, he cut off all contact with me, and I never saw him or spoke to him again.

Mr. Powell always told me he had bequeathed a large number of stocks to me in his will. However, he must have changed his mind after I married, because I was never contacted after his death.

In today's world, we'd have a different view about meeting strangers like Mr. Powell. I'm sure no parent would encourage such a relationship if approached as he did with my mother when I was four. But people were more innocent and trusting back then. Mr. Powell was in my life for twenty years, adding flashes of colour in an otherwise ordinary life. I felt those flashes of colour and enjoyed the excitement. What were his motives? He might have simply been a lonely man who wanted a daughter of his own — or, perhaps more likely, I was a Pygmalion project that never got off the ground. Was he trying to rescue the fair-haired Métis girl from a life of poverty? Did my intuition save me from a life of sadness, or was I a naïve little girl without enough sense to see what he was offering?

My relationship with Mr. Powell is one of the biggest mysteries of my life. What was it all about? I still think about Mr. Powell often and thank him for opening up my small world. Whatever Mr. Powell's motives were, that moment of decision about living with him represents a major crossroads in my life, where the road not travelled would have been much different from the one I chose. I may have a lot of unanswered questions, but I have no regrets. I'm grateful to him for bringing some excitement into my sheltered life and giving me a small peek at a much bigger world … a world I would eventually be eager to explore.

Part Two (1961–1977)

I am a dreamer made real by virtue of the world touching me.

— Richard Wagamese, *Embers*

CHAPTER 7

Coming of Age

I loved my job as a long-distance telephone operator, which paid thirty-six dollars a week. Even by 1961 standards, it wasn't a lot of money, but it was about the same as a bank teller made at the time. My family was now living on the second and third floors of an old duplex on Cedar Street in Sudbury. Mom got a job at Silverman's Department Store, and she was happy to be back where she'd worked before she got married. Dad was still a janitor at the CPR station. My brother and two sisters were all still in school, and I was the only one working besides my parents.

My dad had become a different father to my youngest sister, Maureen, than he'd been with Bruce, Estelle, and me. He took her everywhere with him. They went grocery shopping together, and he had lunch ready for her when he was home on school days. He'd dictate letters for her to write to his sister in Chicago and take her with him to visit friends in Britt. I'd never experienced anything like that with him. I think when we were that age, it was a different time, with my father immersed in the shock of his disability and going through so many adjustments.

But Dad did spend more time with Bruce than with his daughters. Estelle and I were always on the swing or doing girly stuff, so maybe he balanced it out by doing boy stuff with my brother. They did chores together, and he taught Bruce how drive a boat and manoeuvre the dangerous shoals in Georgian Bay. He showed him all the best fishing holes and taught him the Métis way of cleaning his catch. Even with a hook for a left hand, Dad could fillet the boniest fish to perfection.

A decade later, when an unexpected baby girl arrived, perhaps Dad was ready to take on a more active role with her than he had with my sister and me. He established a special relationship with Maureen, and she adored him. There was no jealousy with the rest of us; by that time, we were all older and engrossed in our own teenage dramas.

\+\+\+

The place where we lived wasn't a fancy apartment, and the owner was an old man who lived downstairs. He was a heavy drinker who wore spats and a top hat and carried a walking stick when he went out. He looked like a caricature of W. C. Fields. We didn't have a lot of furniture, but there were enough bedrooms for all of us. I shared a room on the third floor with my sister Estelle, and Bruce and Maureen had rooms down the hall.

I remember the place had cockroaches and how they would scatter in the kitchen sink when we turned on the light. Before that, the only place I'd seen cockroaches was in the woodpile in Britt. Despite the bugs, it was home, and I was happy my family was together again. I paid fifteen dollars a week for room and board and enjoyed my freedom from the constraints that Marymount had placed on me. Relieved to be out of my dowdy school tunic and black oxfords, I spent almost every cent I earned on clothes.

After I completed my training, Bell started off my career with a recruitment publicity campaign. They used me as a model for attracting new recruits to the switchboard, as the telephone business was growing rapidly. I was on human resource advertisements inserted into monthly telephone bills for their customers. And on one occasion, I was asked to appear on a morning television show in Sudbury with the human resources manager to talk about my job. All this attention was exciting for a sixteen-year-old, and I learned quickly. I was trained to operate a PBX switchboard, handling long-distance calls and some local calls for small towns without home telephones, as we used to have in Britt. We wore headsets, and I sat in a long row of telephone operators, each with our own board consisting of fifteen to twenty cords and a clock to time our calls for billing. We managed several customers at one time, keeping our eyes on the blinking lights to make sure we answered and ended calls on time. I loved the job and took to it immediately.

We were a roomful of sixties' switchboard girls, with bouffant hairdos, breath-crunching girdles, and silky nylon stockings with black seams up the back. Pants, or slacks as they were called then, were not allowed at work.

I felt good about myself, having finally found a place outside of my Britt community where I fit in and excelled at something. Within one year, I became a supervisor and training instructor. Life couldn't be better.

+++

I often worked evenings, and Bell paid for a taxi home if we worked past twelve-thirty. But many afternoon shifts ended before that, and on those evenings, I would walk home. One night, after working a split shift that ended at ten o'clock, I started my walk home when I noticed a red car idling along beside me. I ignored it and kept walking. This continued to happen for a few nights, and I felt uncomfortable. But I lived only five blocks from work, so when I saw the car, I simply sped up.

At about eleven-fifteen one night, I was a block from my house when the same red car slowed down, then quickly sped up and disappeared. Shortly after, I heard a noise behind me and turned to look. The red car was parked at the curb with the motor running, and a man in a hooded sweatshirt was running toward me. I took off in my high heels and ran quickly for home. I was terrified as I reached the duplex and raced up the front porch stairs, as I could hear his feet on the walkway behind me.

I opened the door to the entrance hall and screamed for my father, who came bounding down the stairs in his grey work socks. I'd never seen Dad move so fast. He chased the man down the street, and the guy made a getaway. But my dad saw the red car he was driving and recognized the vehicle. Turns out it was someone who worked with my father at the CPR. Dad said he had noticed him watching me when I visited him at the station. To this day, I'm not sure what my father did, but he must have taken care of it because I never saw the guy again, and Dad never mentioned it.

+++

Not long after that, I was asleep in my bedroom on the third floor with my window open. I woke up with a start about one in the morning when I heard screaming coming from the street. I looked out and saw a woman struggling with a man on the sidewalk. I saw him punch her in the stomach and drag her between the buildings across the road. I ran downstairs to my parents' bedroom, and we called the police. I couldn't see much of what was happening after that, with all the police cars and flashing red lights. But an officer eventually came to our door and took a statement from me. He said they caught the guy, and I would probably have to testify in court about what I saw. When I returned to my bedroom, Estelle was still asleep. She had slept through the whole thing.

I was unnerved by the incident and tried to trade my early evening shifts as much as I could. But that was hard to do, as most of the girls preferred working the shifts that ended after twelve-thirty so that they could get a free cab ride home.

About a month after that incident, I received a subpoena to appear at the trial. My mom wanted to take the day off work, but I told her my older friend Pauline would come with me. No one in my family had ever been in a courtroom. Mom reluctantly agreed, but little did I know what I was getting myself into.

On the day of the trial, I dressed carefully. I had never been in a courtroom, but I knew enough from watching Perry Mason's legal dramas on TV that I needed to dress well. I wore a new light blue dress with a matching coat, and I could feel the sweat in my armpits when Pauline picked me up.

We sat on a wooden bench in the courtroom until my case was announced. I became even more nervous when I heard the man who attacked the woman say he was representing himself. That meant he would be questioning me, and the thought of facing him made me want to bolt out of there. Pauline held my hand and told me I had to stay.

When I was called up to the stand, the judge asked me how old I was. When I told him I was seventeen, he directed me to look at him and not the defendant during his questions. The attacker was standing close to me on the stand, but I didn't take my eyes off the judge. I spoke so fast when I answered the man's questions that the judge laughed and asked me to slow down, saying he couldn't listen in shorthand. I got through the experience thanks to the kindness of the judge, and I sat back down with Pauline to hear the rest of the trial. That's when things went off the rails.

The judge called the woman who was attacked up to the stand. She had stringy brown hair and wore a pair of baggy pants that hung on her body. Her complexion was sallow, and I couldn't tell her age. I'm not sure why, but the judge took over the questioning and asked the woman to describe what happened that night.

The woman said she was walking along Cedar Street at about one in the morning, heading home to her apartment. The judge interrupted and asked her if she had been drinking, and she replied that she had been drinking beer at the Coulson Hotel. She said the man attacked her from behind, then punched and dragged her between the buildings, where he tried to rape her. At this point, I could feel my face getting hot and my armpits getting wetter. I looked at Pauline, who looked back at me and scrunched up her face.

The woman continued by telling the court what the man did to her as he attempted to rape her. She used crude and graphic words to describe her ordeal, using language I'd never heard before.

I gasped so loud with an "Oh my God!" that everyone, including the judge, turned in my direction. I had my hands over my face, and when I looked up and saw everyone staring at me, I started to cry. To say I had no experience or education in sexual matters would be an understatement. I had a boyfriend, but other than kissing and a bit of light petting, I had only a basic understanding of sex. My parents never discussed such topics with me, and heaven forbid the nuns at Marymount should teach such sinful things.

The judge, seeing my distress, called a recess and asked a court policewoman to take me into the bathroom to calm me down. The poor officer did her best to explain what was going on and gave me a quick bit of sex education right there outside the bathroom stall. Pauline held my hand and tried her best to look serious. There are some experiences in life that never fade, and that was one for me. I still feel sorry for the young, inexperienced girl I was, thrown into that situation so unprepared.

My *True Confessions* magazines were vague in their references to sex, and my favourite movies were *Pillow Talk* and *The Pajama Game*. So that was my point of reference and how romantic I imagined sex to be. And while the information I heard in court was difficult enough for me to understand at the time, the horrors of rape were well beyond anything I knew about. It was all very meshed together and confusing and would stay with me for years.

When I composed myself, we returned to the courtroom, where the trial had already resumed. As soon as I sat down, the judge called my name and told me I could leave, even though the proceedings were still underway. Pauline and I headed for the exit, but before I got there, I felt a tug on my arm. When I turned, I came face to face with the woman who had been attacked. What I remember most about seeing her up close like that was the hollow, sunken look in her eyes and the smell of something sour on her breath.

"Thank you," she said and smiled at me.

I couldn't tell my parents what went on in the courtroom that day. No one but Pauline knew. I was far too embarrassed to talk about it and certain if they knew, Mom and Dad would be upset that they had let me go without them. Or perhaps they would have been relieved not to witness that with me. I didn't even try to find out the verdict of the trial; I just wanted to put it behind me. But as I struggled to keep the bad memories buried, I could still see them vividly in my head. I hoped that over time, the images would fade and leave me alone. Sadly, that didn't happen. I kept reliving the screams I heard in the night, the man questioning me on the stand, the discussion in the bathroom, and the woman's hollow appearance. In my sheltered life, I had never been exposed to this element of society or the ugly violence of rape. It haunted me, and I kept the images trapped in my head; I didn't know how to release them.

✦✦✦

While all this was going on in my personal life, my job was going well, and Bell was ramping up my recruitment role for the company. They asked me to attend a conference in London, Ontario, and I agreed to go. I was the first one in my family to get on an airplane, and Mom tried to talk me out of going. "Way too dangerous," she told me. "Tell them to send someone older."

But I wanted to do this despite feeling a nervous excitement at the prospects of flying and staying in a hotel, which I'd also never done. The flight took a couple of hours — the longest two hours of my life. I sat clutching the arms of my seat, palms soaking wet, and I felt like throwing up. The stewardess could see my distress and handed me a little paper bag from the back of the seat. I loved looking out at the clouds but hated every bump and shudder during the flight. When we finally landed, I was relieved the ordeal was over, but I dreaded the return trip.

I made it through my first hotel experience with just a few embarrassing incidents, like not knowing how to check in to my room and losing the hotel key on the way to my floor. As the youngest one at the conference, I was nervous and on edge during my two days there. But overall, I was glad I went, and I felt grown-up and worldly when I came home with stories to tell my family.

Shortly after that, though, I started to fall apart. When I'd walk home from work, I found myself constantly looking around, reliving the red car incident and being chased down the sidewalk. When I slept, I had nightmares about running for my life, unable to scream, as the man got closer. Sometimes, the man chasing me was the would-be rapist from the courtroom, and my legs felt like they were mired in quicksand as I tried to escape. In some dreams, I was on an airplane as it plunged to the ground and people around me were screaming in terror. During the day, I was irritable and forgetful, and I cried easily. It was starting to affect my job.

Seeing what was happening, my mother sat me down to talk. I wept into my cup of tea while she calmly explained I'd been through a lot in a short time — although she still didn't know the details of what happened in the courtroom. Mom said they had found a house to rent in a safer neighbourhood away from downtown, and we would be moving there the following month. She also insisted on taking me to see our family doctor about what I was going through.

Dr. White responded to my anxiety issues as many doctors did in the 1960s: he prescribed pills. He gave me tranquilizers to take three times a day to calm me down and amphetamines to take twice a day to improve my mood. I took the drug cocktail of uppers and downers as he prescribed and found myself crying hysterically one minute and laughing uncontrollably the next. In between, I was mostly comatose. I begged my mother to let me come off the pills, but she said the doctor knew best and I should take them as directed. After two weeks, I decided the cure was worse than the disease, and I threw all the pills in the garbage. I was determined to get through this without drugs.

The first thing I decided to do was talk about it. I called Pauline and asked her to meet me at the Radio Lunch for a Coke. For the first time, we discussed that day in the courtroom. Pauline was a good listener, but she could also see the humour in everything. She helped me to feel safe again by talking about it and bringing a lightheartedness to what I was feeling. Over a plate of french fries with gravy, we found ourselves laughing until we cried. The humour was more about my reaction and not the court case itself, which was scary and sad. What happened was traumatizing, but the giggles with Pauline helped me to soften the feelings of being trapped in my memories. It felt good to lift the lid and release the pressure. Once that part was over, things got easier. When I began to feel anxious at work, I'd go into a bathroom stall to breathe and calm down. At home, I listened to music or sat on our lawn swing to make myself relax. Rocking has always done that for me, from the time I was a child in my grandmother Charron's rocking chair in the kitchen.

Over the next couple of months, my anxiety lessened, and the dreams and flashbacks stopped. That experience would be the start of my lifelong aversion to taking prescribed drugs and a deep mistrust of the medical profession still with me today.

Over the following three years, I continued to enjoy my work as a long-distance supervisor and training instructor and had fewer recruitment assignments. I specifically remember the afternoon of November 22, 1963. I was standing behind a new trainee, with my headset on listening to her calls, when a customer told her that John Kennedy had been shot. Like everyone else who remembers that day, it was a moment in time I will never forget. I didn't follow politics, but like many young women, I loved Jackie Kennedy and her beautiful style of dressing. I'd heard President Kennedy speak on television — they looked like the perfect couple. I found it horrifying that someone would assassinate him. Later that day when I got home, we all crowded around the television to watch replay after replay of the car scene on the street when he was shot. It didn't seem real.

✦✦✦

My family was living in a lovely house on Park Road, about ten minutes by bus to downtown Sudbury. Bruce was now working at Woolworth's while Estelle attended Marymount, and my youngest sister, Maureen, was in a Catholic elementary school. We were all together, and at twenty, I felt safe and secure, with no big drama in my life.

One day, I was coming back to work after shopping during my lunch hour. The wind was blowing hard, and dirt devils swirled around me on the sidewalk. I was attempting to hold on to my skirt, my lacquered coif, and my shopping bags when I opened the door to the Bell building. Just as I did, a huge gust of wind grabbed the door and flung it wide open, pulling me off balance and right into the chest of a man coming out at the same time.

"Whoa! This is my lucky day," he said, as he steadied me. I looked up into the face of Mister Tall, Dark, and Dreamy. Fate had literally thrown us together, like a romantic scene right out of my *True Love* magazine. Rick Nadon had burst into my life.

CHAPTER 8

Stand By Your Man

Rick was only a year older than I but had lived a much different life. He joined the army at the age of sixteen and had just returned from a two-year posting as a signalman at the most northerly inhabited place in the world: Canadian Forces Station (CFS) Alert, Ellesmere Island, Northwest Territories. After that frigid assignment, where he had to tie himself to a building to venture outside in the howling wind and blowing snow, he was ready to get out of the army. After five years' service, Rick received his discharge and accepted a job at Bell Telephone in Sudbury as a technician in the mechanical equipment room, downstairs from where I worked.

I fell hard and fast for his winning charm and incredibly good looks. Rick drove a small blue MGB, was always impeccably dressed, and made me laugh with his infectious sense of humour. He was definitely the coolest guy I'd ever met. He was a dreamer and wanted to do big things in his life. I found that exciting. I was thrilled someone as handsome as Rick picked me for a girlfriend. He asked me to marry him a week after our first date, and while he caught me off guard, I said yes three days later.

Rick came from a family of heavy drinkers, so it was part of who he was. He took to alcohol at an early age to look for acceptance at home. But at sixteen, during a drinking binge, he had a huge fist fight with his dad and left home. That's when he joined the army, where there was often nothing to do at night but drink with his buddies. So, this level of drinking had been going on for years.

Rick was easy in the company of both men and women. I was happy to stand back and watch him charm the room. He never returned the attention of the many women who flirted with him. Sometimes when he drank too much, especially rum, his mood would turn ugly, and he would look for a fist fight with any man who looked at him the wrong way. I avoided eye contact with him during those episodes in case he aimed his anger at me. That should have triggered some warning bells, but I was madly and blindly in love. He was just a good old boy from Northern Ontario, I told myself. When he wasn't drinking, he made me laugh and feel special. I had no experience with men like Rick, so I assumed his behaviour was normal. I thought I simply needed to grow up and learn how to live with it if I wanted to keep him. I was sure his temperament would settle down once we were married.

We set a wedding date for the following August, only nine months after we met. On my twenty-first birthday, the March before the wedding, Rick was in an accident with his dad's car and charged with drunk driving. I was at home with my parents, where I was still living until we got married. Mom and Dad were not impressed when he finally arrived at our door in a cab at midnight.

After he left, my parents said they were very worried about his drinking. But in those days, drinking and driving was a more acceptable thing for some people, and I made his excuses and dismissed their concerns. I wanted to marry this exciting man who drove a sports car and swept me off my feet. That was all that mattered. I didn't think someone like me could ever find anyone more exciting to be with than Rick. He was such a handsome man and he wanted to be with me … the little girl from Britt. In my mind, only popular girls got to date men like that. I didn't want to lose him; I needed to make it work.

The wedding was all planned. We invited one hundred and twenty-five guests to our reception at the Sorrento Hotel in Sudbury on August 13, 1966. The night before the big day, I was at home with my family packing clothes for my honeymoon. I felt giddy with excitement and anticipation. The phone rang, and it was the Sudbury Police, asking for my father. Rick had been thrown in jail after a drunken bar brawl, and he was asking for my father to bail him out. All the joy I was feeling drained out of my body. My dad wouldn't let me go with him, but he reluctantly bailed Rick out of jail and took him back to his apartment. After Dad came home, I'll never forget the scene when I walked into the kitchen.

My mild-mannered father was sitting in a chair shaking his head and pounding his fist on the kitchen table. "We can't let her marry that guy, Laura."

Mom was blowing her nose and crying. "How it starts is most likely how it will end," she said.

They tried to talk to me, but I would hear none of it. I was crazy in love, and I insisted he would change. I went to bed the night before my wedding day, crying into my pillow. Nothing up to that point in my life had prepared me to cope with a man like Rick. I felt swallowed up by the enormity of it all, but cancelling the wedding wasn't an option I wanted to consider.

I think of that now and imagine putting myself in my parents' place. How they must have suffered. I try to imagine how I would feel going through this with my daughter or granddaughter. As parents, we only have so much influence over the decisions our children make when they become adults. We hope by giving them a good foundation, they will choose wisely. But despite the good intentions of my mom and dad, my foundation wasn't as solid as it should have been. I didn't think enough of myself to have the courage to walk away.

✦✦✦

The next day Rick and I were married — me in a virginal white dress and veil, and my handsome groom in a tuxedo, sporting a broken nose and a black eye. Despite Rick's injuries, the wedding was a lovely affair, and I was grateful to my parents for supporting me on my big day. Rick's parents thought getting married with a smashed-up face was funny and had a good laugh about it. But they spent most Saturdays at the local Royal Canadian Legion knocking back draft beer and had seen their share of fights. But my parents didn't find it funny, and I just didn't want to think about it. Rick was the man of my dreams, I told myself. He loved me, and once we were married, everything would be different. It's what married men did: they settled down and became respectable. I heard other girls at Bell talking about their marriages. No husband was perfect, and neither would mine be. All perfectly normal, I convinced myself.

Mom told me only three things about finding the right man: always have your own bank account; remember the power of novenas to help in a crisis; and never trust a man who wears an ascot. I'm not sure where she got that last one, but it came in handy a decade later.

My wedding night was not what I expected. We checked into the Mandarin Motor Hotel in town, and Rick fell asleep as soon as we got to our room, after drinking his way through the reception. I spent the night looking out the window, feeling drained of the happiness I'd felt all day. I was a naïve twenty-one-year-old virgin who believed every word of what I read in my romance magazines. I wasn't experienced in sex, but I was a willing participant to find out. Unfortunately, my first lesson in married life was to discover that real life was nothing like what I read in glossy magazines.

Before the wedding, Rick told me we would be honeymooning for a week at the Gray Rocks Resort in Mont Tremblant, Quebec, which I was excited about. However, when we got on the road the next day, despite the cash we got for wedding gifts, he said we didn't have enough money to go there and would have to change our plans. We went as far as Saint-Hubert, Quebec, and stayed in a strip motel. There were two single beds in the room. Rick moved the nightstand and pushed the beds together, which made me feel anxious and excited at the same time. After we unpacked, I took a shower and flooded the motel bathroom because I didn't put the shower curtain inside the tub.

That night, Rick and I had sex for the first time. I found it painful, messy, and over very quickly. After all the buildup, it wasn't what I expected — like when electricity came to Britt, there were none of the coloured lights I was expecting. After a couple of days, our honeymoon was cut short because we ran out of money and had to go home.

✦✦✦

Over the next eight years, we moved twelve times back and forth between different Ontario cities and towns: Sudbury, Levack, North Bay, Ottawa, and Toronto. Rick was always in pursuit of a better job or business opportunity and had dreams of making it big. He was a smart guy, with an infectious sense of humour and an ability to win people over easily. But the drinking would always ruin whatever he was striving to achieve, and he would self-destruct.

I hid our problems and the empty bottles from my family when they visited. I even made excuses for Rick when he humiliated my father by bouncing a cheque at Begins General Store in Britt. I lied to cover for him when he was AWOL on a drinking binge, and I followed him like a loyal little wife in all our moves. I convinced myself that I loved this man and never considered a life beyond that. When he was sober, he was affectionate and charming, and said all the right things. By that time, I was working as a service representative in the Bell business office, and the company was usually able to provide me with transfers to keep up with my moving from place to place.

Rick was fun to be around, and he treated me well when he wasn't drunk. I give him credit for never pressuring me to drink with him. Most of his boozing was done without me in bars, and I was left alone to worry about him. When he did come home, he was all apologetic and affectionate. But the smell of booze on him made me gag, and I pushed him away until he passed out. The next day, he was always contrite, and his wicked laugh softened my anger. Despite the bar brawls, the drunken rages, and the restlessness he brought to our marriage, I believed he loved me and that someday he would change. I was desperate to make it work.

My mom always told Estelle and me that a woman should never put up with physical abuse. She often repeated this and said, "If they hit you once, they'll do it again." That seemed to be the marriage deal-breaker for her. Rick never hurt me physically, and I was certain he didn't cheat on me with other women. I never once considered leaving him. I would stand by my man, as my mother had stood by my father.

Although my challenges with Rick's drinking were very different from what my mom had endured, she'd been stoic in her duties to our family and had survived hardships living in Britt and not liking it there. I thought things had worked out fine for her, and I believed I'd be fine too. Plus, what was my alternative? Losing him and being alone? I'd much rather stay with him in his world than set out to discover my own. Besides, I wouldn't know where to start. I rationalized it all by believing the good times outweighed the bad. But down deep, I was afraid to be alone, afraid I would never find someone else who would love me, and afraid to face my parents with the truth about my marriage. My inability to confront myself about the truth of what was happening chained me to the relationship.

✦✦✦

Four years after we were married, we moved from Ottawa back to Sudbury. We rented the top floor of a new triplex. On August 20, 1970, the day after the moving truck arrived, we were both at work when a deadly tornado bore down on the city. The effects were devastating. When we arrived home, we could see blue sky through our bedroom window. The tornado had peeled the roof back, and our apartment was open to the elements. We climbed the stairs, and I felt such despair when I felt our new carpets squishing under my feet and saw our furniture toppled and broken. Most of our clothes were in boxes drenched with rain.

We stayed with my sister Estelle and her husband, John, in their small basement apartment while we looked for another place to live. But because of the city-wide destruction, there was nothing available. We made the decision to move in with Rick's parents, Roly and Gert, in Levack, a mining town about forty-five minutes from Sudbury. Rick's father, Roly, worked at the Inco mine, and they lived in a company house there. We had a small bedroom off the kitchen.

Although his parents were drinkers, they were mostly good to both of us. His mom was Irish and always pressured me to have a drink to "loosen up," she'd tell me. She called me "Kitten" because she said I was timid like one. She told me I should let out my emotions, scream, yell, and throw things. That didn't make any sense to me with the upbringing I'd had, and it frightened me to hear her say that. But I simply laughed and shrugged it off. The weekends were the worst. I couldn't handle the drunken arguments. When the drinking began, big disagreements would start, and so did the yelling. Anything could trigger it. I would sit upstairs in the bathroom shaking and crying until eventually someone stormed out of the house, and it stopped.

+++

We were still living with Rick's parents, looking for our own place, when I got pregnant. It was an unexpected development because I was on the pill. I was frightened about my future without my own home for the baby. I felt panicky when I thought too much about it. It was the first time I wondered if my marriage would last, and I worried what kind of a father my husband would be. But Rick and his parents made such a big fuss about my pregnancy, so I settled down and began looking forward to having a child. I was still with Bell, and Rick had a job with Avco Financial Services.

Then, my husband decided he would open two businesses in Levack: a pizzeria franchise and a dry-cleaning store, Sparkle Cleaners. He had no experience in either one. Life was about to get even more complicated. He borrowed money from friends and family to get his enterprises going and promised them a big rate of return on their investment. He hired staff, and his mother worked the cash register at the dry cleaner's.

Rick rented a van to do deliveries for the cleaner's and worked part-time at the pizza place.

My mom and I shopped for patterns and fabric, and she made me a beautiful maternity wardrobe of pantsuits and dresses. Rick and I finally found a place to rent in Sudbury and moved in when I was about five months pregnant. It went well enough at first, but it didn't last.

Rick travelled to Levack every day to keep the businesses going. I began getting calls at home from customers looking for their dry cleaning. They would scream at me and say they'd seen the Sparkle Cleaners van parked outside the local hotel all afternoon. Rick would come home late, sometimes with incoherent excuses, sometimes barely able to walk. Despite it all, he managed to keep both businesses going, and I stayed with him. I was pregnant, so what else was there for me to do? I never had any fear of him for my own safety and felt only relief when he came home.

I experienced Braxton Hicks contractions for two weeks before the doctor decided to induce labour. On July 10, 1971, Rick drove me to the hospital, and I wouldn't let him stay in the room. Mostly because it was the way things were back then, but also because I had attended the prenatal classes alone. So, I didn't know how he could help me if he stayed. After fourteen hours of natural birthing contractions, my beautiful baby Andrea came into the world at 11:50 p.m. I instantly adored all seven pounds, eleven ounces of her. Of course, my sister Estelle and her husband, John, would be her godparents.

CHAPTER 9

How Can You Mend a Broken Heart?

I remained in the hospital for a week, which was normal in those days. When Rick visited, he fussed and cooed over the baby, but I couldn't help but notice he was unshaven and smelling of booze. When my husband picked us up to go home, he looked tired and his eyes were bloodshot. I was already feeling anxious because Andrea was a fussy baby, and Mom wasn't arriving to help me until the next day. Rick was not very talkative on the way home. When I asked him if something was wrong, he said he was having some business problems and might have to declare bankruptcy. I felt like vomiting.

There's a scene in my head from that first day home with Andrea I won't ever forget. I was sitting in a black leather rocking chair in the living room, holding my sleeping baby. Rick was on the phone in the kitchen, and I could see him standing there in nothing but his white underwear, his face getting redder and his voice getting louder. He was trying to convince one of his investors in the pizzeria to float him a loan so that the business wouldn't go under. It obviously wasn't going well.

A few minutes later, he was screaming into the phone and jumping up and down like a child throwing a temper tantrum. The receiver was connected to the wall by a long-coiled cord, and he threw it on the floor with a crash. I watched it bounce around the kitchen before the mouthpiece fell off. Andrea woke with a start and began to howl. In the background, the Bee Gees were singing "How Can You Mend a Broken Heart," and I sobbed into my little baby's head.

I was frightened to see him in such a state. There was my Prince Charming in full view — his fear, his frustration, his volatility, and his failures. And in that moment, they became mine too. It took me twenty years to be able to listen to that beautiful song without reliving the despair I felt on that day.

♦♦♦

The next few months were no better. Rick lost the pizzeria but managed to hang on to the cleaners. He was often absent, and I was alone with the baby with no money and sometimes no food. The landlord came to the door every day asking for Rick. We were behind in the rent, but the poor man must have taken pity on me because he never once asked me for money. Estelle and I talked almost daily about my marriage, and while we both knew things were bad, neither one of us brought up the option of my leaving him. Estelle was my sister and best friend, and I told her everything. She never judged, only offered support and a haven if we ever needed a place to stay. Andrea was her goddaughter, and I knew she loved us both.

One day I called her, frantic because Rick hadn't come home for a couple of days. I had no food for me or the baby, and no money, not even coins to wash the diapers. Within the hour, my sister and her husband arrived with groceries, baby formula, and a bag of quarters and dimes for the laundry. I was humiliated but grateful for the help. I had weird cravings during that difficult time and lived on chocolate cake and grape pop, which they'd included in their shopping list. My baby still had colic, but looking back, how could she not, with the stress in our home as thick as disappointment?

When Andrea was about three months old, I got up with her at six in the morning, and I heard a noise coming from the living room closet. I opened the door and saw my drunken husband sitting on the floor mumbling incoherently with his shirt ripped and streaked with blood. I managed to get him to bed, where he stayed for the rest of the day. He wouldn't tell me where he'd been.

After that incident, I had my first thoughts about leaving him. How could I allow this man to be a father to my baby? I worried about the kind of environment she would grow up in, the disappointments and hurt she would endure. It was terrifying to think of myself alone with a new baby, maybe even ending up on welfare. I argued with myself. How could I possibly survive without a man in my life? Just the thought of it gave me heart palpitations and stomach cramps. I wanted to leave but didn't know how. Soon after, when Rick stayed away for another two days, I had more time to think as I paced the floor with my colicky baby. I had to do this for Andrea and me.

I contacted a girlfriend I had in Ottawa from my Bell Telephone working days there. I filled her in on what I was planning to do and told her I was coming in on a bus the next day, asking if I could stay with her for a bit. I was going to see about getting my old job back in the Bell offices there. The distance from Rick would be good and a fresh start with Andrea would be even better, I told her. Huguette agreed, happy I was finally going to leave him. My plan was to get my mother-in-law, Gert, to take care of the baby for a few days while I was in Ottawa. Gert had stopped drinking when Andrea was born, and I trusted her to be with my daughter. I didn't pre-arrange it with her because I knew she'd try to talk me out of leaving her son. I would drop Andrea off on my way to the bus depot, confident in knowing any opportunity to take her granddaughter would be welcomed. She adored Andrea. I went to bed that night with my suitcase packed, my hair up in rollers, and terrified about what I was going to do.

At around four in the morning, the phone woke me. It was my brother-in-law John. He said Rick was in the hospital, and he needed to take me there while Estelle stayed with the baby. I told him I didn't care where Rick was; I didn't want to see him. He pleaded with me, saying my husband was in rough shape. Apparently, he had come to the aid of a woman being harassed by a biker in a bar outside of town. Unfortunately, the biker and the rest of his motorcycle gang didn't appreciate Rick's attempt at chivalry. They beat him up pretty badly, then roared away on their Harleys and left him bleeding on the sidewalk. I reluctantly agreed to go to the hospital with my brother-in-law.

As John and I were getting on the elevator at the hospital, a nurse was stepping off with a man crumpled in a wheelchair. I stepped past them just as John said, "Rick?" I looked back and could see the man in the wheelchair was my husband. His face was barely recognizable, swollen and caked with dried blood, one eye only partially open. He had bandages on both hands, and there was a large bald patch on the left side of his head where his hair had been ripped out. He was having trouble looking up to see who had called his name. My stomach lurched, and my knees turned to rubber. The room spun as black spots inked my eyesight. I leaned on John for support. We followed the nurse to his room, but Rick was heavily sedated and barely acknowledged we were there.

In the end, I felt sorry for him and lost my nerve to leave him when he was in that state. I wanted to be hopeful. Maybe he'd learned a lesson. Maybe this would finally scare him into changing. Maybe we could make it work after all. My courage drained away, and I scrapped all my big plans to leave. Was I looking for an excuse to stay? Would I have gone through with it? I'll never know, but I ended up enjoying the best two weeks I'd had for years because Gert and Roly insisted Andrea and I stay with them while Rick was in hospital. I sighed with gratitude and agreed.

For the first time in years, I didn't have to worry about where Rick was; he was safe and sober in a hospital. The comfort of being taken care of was a welcome respite. I put my life on hold, and for a short time, I stopped worrying about money, Rick's drinking, and my future.

Andrea settled down, sleeping more and crying less. She was already laughing out loud, bouncing a bit in her infant swing, and she was strong enough to roll over in her crib. She was the centre of my universe and the one bright spot that filled my heart every day. My calm environment gave me time to think. Estelle and I talked often, and I told her I was sure this experience would make Rick stop drinking. I emphasized the tenderness and love he showed Andrea and me during his sober times. Despite everything, I insisted, he was a decent man and our marriage wasn't so bad. I knew her well enough to know she wasn't convinced, but I talked myself into staying. Estelle just hugged me and gave me a key to her apartment.

+++

When Rick recovered, things got a bit better for a while. His drinking was more under control, and Sparkle Cleaners was doing okay. But soon enough, the old patterns emerged, and I had the landlord pounding on my door. It was about that time I started to write poetry as a way to release the emotions I was feeling. Most of it was depressing stuff, but I also wrote about the only real joy in my life, my beautiful daughter. I was thrilled when I had my first poem published in *Best Wishes*, a magazine for new mothers.

+++

The intimate part of our relationship changed after Andrea was born. Rick stopped having any sexual interest in me. At first, I didn't care because I was exhausted taking care of the baby and surviving all Rick's dramas. But over time, I felt hurt and blamed myself for not doing enough to keep him interested. The truth was I didn't want to get pregnant again anyway. So, I rationalized it and tried to ignore the fact that there was no intimacy left between us. We slept in the same bed, but that was all. I hung on to the hope that things would change when Rick found the dream he was always chasing: the dream to make it big.

Rick eventually had to shut down the dry cleaners and declare bankruptcy. I found it difficult to be around the family and friends who had lent him money. There was a lot of resentment and disagreements because they never got a cent of their investment back. I found the constant conflict suffocating.

We moved again and again and again as Rick took various jobs until we landed in Toronto. My restless husband decided he wanted to go back to school and was accepted as a mature student at York University. We sold everything we owned and moved to a furnished apartment on the top floor of the graduate student residence. Andrea was nearly two years old. I got a job on campus in the admissions office, and I found a great babysitter. I liked going to work, but at the same time, I was depressed and having dark thoughts about taking my life. It was very real and disturbing, following me through my days. I had visions of stepping out onto the roof of my apartment building, eighteen floors up, and simply letting myself fly over the side.

It was a painful time, but I never discussed those feelings with my husband. He was entrenched in university life and kept himself busy with his studies and new friends. And even Estelle, who I'd always been so close to, didn't know what I was going through. She was still living in Sudbury, which was a long way from Toronto, and I had no money for long discussions on the phone.

I saw a psychologist at the university for a while, and with his help, I managed myself through it. In the end, it was my love for Andrea that kept me together and gave me purpose. I couldn't bear to think of the pain I would cause by leaving her ... especially leaving her with Rick.

I suspected my husband had a life outside of Andrea and me. He was away many nights, and I'd heard rumours from my colleagues at York about a woman he'd been seen with. I avoided bringing up the subject with him because I couldn't face the answer I knew was waiting for me. Probably the usual lies, but just maybe the truth. I felt so alone and lonely for companionship.

I remember one Saturday evening, sitting quietly with my daughter in the rooftop lounge of the university apartment building. We were alone up there, and Andrea was asleep with her head in my lap. As I looked out at the night lights of the Toronto skyline, I picked up my poetry journal and wrote, *Loneliness is love cracked down the middle. Artificial glue will not withstand the test of time.* When I think of that moment, I can still feel the raw emotions in my chest.

It shouldn't have come as a surprise when school finished in the spring and Rick left me to move in with Tanya, a woman he met in one of his classes. I'd met her once at my job at the university, without knowing about the relationship. She was the opposite of me — outgoing, wealthy, and confident. Tanya was a mature student with an apartment in the university residence and a home in Yorkville. I knew Rick and I had grown apart, but despite everything, I felt broken.

♦♦♦

When summer was over, Rick and Tanya had a falling-out, and he came back to live with Andrea and me for the next semester. While I felt like a doormat by accepting him back, I couldn't consider what my alternative might be, not having any money or another place to go.

Perhaps I took Rick back because I hoped he'd learned something over the summer too; maybe he'd realized how important Andrea and I were to him. Although I felt humiliated by the betrayal, I was too afraid to confront him about Tanya. I didn't want him to leave for good. I still struggle to reconcile who I was back then — a woman without a voice. I'm ashamed I was so weak and thought so little of myself. Taking the easy way out and not creating a scene had become my pattern. I simply didn't know how to fight back.

Rick didn't drink much when we were at York, but there were always women, well hidden from me but still there. Friends I worked with would tell me when they saw him with young female students in campus bars and huddled together in the cafeteria. I once found a picture of a young woman in my tea towel drawer. It was signed "Love, Jocelyn." I wondered if he'd put it there for me to find. I asked him about it, and he said it was a silly young girl in his class who had a crush on him. It was nothing, he said, and I threw it in the garbage.

Rick's passion for university life soon waned, and he found another dream to chase. He was a smooth talker and a big ideas guy, so he never had any trouble finding investors for a new business enterprise. I went along with it all, as usual, wanting desperately to believe in him and his big dreams.

So, with a pile of other people's money, we rented a beautiful house in the prestigious area of Avenue Road, and he opened up Information Please in downtown Toronto. It was a service company that made recommendations and reservations at restaurants and bars in Toronto and several resorts in cottage country. We had a staff of twenty people, including me. But like everything else, it went bust within six months. Rick's drinking always came first, and very soon into the venture, he was back in bars instead of managing the business.

I remember the awful day I had to face our employees when we couldn't meet payroll, and Rick was nowhere to be found. He'd left me to deal with a room full of people looking for their paycheques. I threw up in the toilet before telling them we had no money to pay them. I would think of that moment often in the years to come when I faced difficult work situations. Employees deserved the right to hear the truth.

Not long after that, Rick's Corvette was repossessed from our driveway in the middle of the night. What a racket they made hooking it up to the tow truck as Rick screamed at them through our bedroom window. I can only imagine what the neighbours thought, but I was glad to see that car go. Who drives a sports car with no back seat when you have a baby? We were behind on the rent there too, so we moved again, this time to Ottawa where, ironically, he got a job working for Creditel of Canada, a national collection company.

+++

Rick left for Ottawa ahead of Andrea and me and rented another beautiful home in the community of Blackburn Hamlet. Despite his financial woes, he was always able to talk his way through any credit checks. I eventually followed him with the moving van and our daughter. We had this routine down to a fine art by now. I got a job again in the Bell business office, and Rick did very well at Creditel. Life was peaceful, he wasn't drinking much, and we paid the rent on time.

+++

Rick was a smart man with a good brain for business, despite his personal failures. In 1975, only a year after he started, he was offered a regional manager posting with Creditel in Vancouver. At the same time, I was offered my first management position with Bell. When I came home bursting with my big news, Rick came home with his even bigger news about his job offer in Vancouver. I had a decision to make.

This was my chance to get out of my marriage and make it on my own with Andrea. I agonized about what to do, and Rick suspected I was dragging my feet on following him this time. A few weeks before, my dad had suffered a heart attack, and I visited him in the hospital. I felt the sadness of a child when I saw him in there, reminding me of when he came home after losing his hand. He was recuperating, but his prognosis was still unclear. So, I was also worried about leaving to go so far away from him and my family.

I talked to my mom, who was not happy about my leaving. British Columbia was like another planet to her. Estelle tried her best to convince me to take the Bell job and stay in Ottawa. "This is your big chance to get out," she insisted. In the end, I ignored my family's advice and hoped living on the west coast would be an exciting new start for us. With a big job title to keep him busy, I was hopeful he would stay focused on his work and stop the drinking.

I told Rick we would follow him to Vancouver. I made this decision alone, without discussing last chances with him. There were no confrontations or admonitions, no telling him that Andrea and I deserved better. I still hadn't found my voice or my own self-worth.

CHAPTER 10

The Wild West

Rick left for British Columbia in June 1975 to start his new job while I gave Bell my notice and arranged for the move. The plan was for my daughter and me to leave on the train in early August. Other than following Mr. Powell's travels as a child, I knew nothing of the world outside of Ontario. I was pumped with excitement.

Andrea and I loved our private compartment on the train. It had two bunk beds, a couple of reclining seats, and a bathroom. Andrea was a good traveller; she didn't complain once about the confinements of living on a train. There was comfort in the steady rhythm of the tracks, and I felt nothing but joy to be sharing this journey with my little girl. The closer we were to arriving in British Columbia, the more excited I became about starting our new life in such a faraway place. I felt certain I'd made the right decision to go.

When we arrived, Rick picked us up at the station, and we stayed at the Denby Arms Hotel in downtown Vancouver because he hadn't yet found a place for us to live. We enjoyed our evening as a family, having dinner together in the hotel dining room and catching up. The next morning, Rick went to work, and I planned to take Andrea down to the beach at English Bay. But before we left, I called my dad and wished him a happy birthday. He'd been released from the hospital and was recovering at home. Dad said he was okay, but I could hear the strain in his voice, and he sounded weak.

I was thinking about my dad and his love for the water when Andrea and I walked along the seawall at English Bay. We sat on the beach and drew pictures in the sand. When we returned to the hotel, there was a message at the front desk to call my aunt Bernice. I thought she was calling to wish us well on our move, but when I returned her call, it was something very different. My father had suffered another heart attack and died on his sixty-fifth birthday. I felt stunned and hollow inside, unable to believe what she was telling me. I had just spoken to him a few hours before, and now I would never see him again. So, a little more than twenty-four hours after we arrived in Vancouver, Andrea and I boarded a red-eye flight to go back home.

+++

Mom and Dad had retired from their jobs in Sudbury several years earlier and had been back living in our old house in Britt. If Mom had had her way, they would never have returned, but Dad was intent on going back, and she finally agreed. Andrea and I made our way to Britt to help Mom through the adjustment. We ended up staying for two months. There was a lot to do, with helping her sell Dad's boat and car, and sending out thank-you notes to friends and family for their thoughtfulness. My brother's wife, Ann, was invaluable during this time. She was like a daughter to my mom and dad.

My family were all grieving, and while we missed our father, it was my youngest sister, Maureen, who was having the most difficulty. After the three of us got married, she was left living at home like an only child. Now, Maureen was married and living hours away in Oshawa, worrying about Mom.

I was reluctant to leave my mother alone, especially with the colder months approaching. At Estelle and John's urging, she agreed to move in with them for the winter. But even then, I continued to drag my feet about going west. I couldn't use Mom as my excuse anymore. Despite the sadness of the situation, life with her in Britt was calm and predictable. Andrea and I needed calm and predictable; we were happy there. And for the first time, my mother suggested I leave my husband.

She asked, "Do you really want to follow Rick to the other side of the world?" Mom said Sudbury would be a great place for Andrea and me to have a good life, surrounded by family. I had to admit it was an appealing thought. She planned on selling the house and moving to an apartment there in a couple of years, which was something she'd always wanted to do.

Estelle came down from Sudbury most weekends while I was there. She didn't push me in any direction, just listened to what I had to say. "You have to do what feels right for you," she'd tell me when we were alone in our old bedroom upstairs. My sister was always the diplomat, something she inherited from Mom. I loved her so much for being there and letting me work it out.

Rick telephoned me many times while I was in Britt, anxious to know when Andrea and I were coming back out west. He told me he bought a split-level house for us in Coquitlam, a suburb of Vancouver, and was taking possession at the end of September. I had no idea where he got the money for the down payment and naïvely didn't ask. Every time we talked, he was sober and said all the right things, telling me how beautiful it was out there and how good our life would be. I kept stalling until finally he asked me outright if I planned to return at all.

I wondered why he wanted us out there so badly and came to the realization it was to see his daughter. By that time, we'd been in a sexless marriage for four years. I let myself wonder if a fresh start far away from all the bad memories would give us a chance to find each other again.

Bottom line: going with him was, once again, the easy way out. Yes, the ground was always shaking in my life with Rick, but I felt a black hole opening in front of me whenever I thought of leaving him. I wanted to believe he would succeed, that he would change and we would be all right. So, late in October, Andrea and I said goodbye to my family and boarded a plane for Vancouver.

+++

It was exciting to move into a beautiful house at the foot of a mountain and settle into new place. Rick loved music as much as I did, and we spent many evenings as a family blasting the new stereo he'd purchased, playing Neil Diamond, Chicago, the Eagles, and Bob Dylan. He snuggled his daughter and gave her the love and kisses she'd missed when we were away with my mom.

I was thrilled when our new neighbour, Jim, who was an RCMP officer, offered to teach me to drive. After I got my licence, Rick got me a car — a metallic lime green Chevrolet Monza with a white vinyl roof. I began to feel free and more independent. It was a new experience for me, and I felt like I'd grown wings. Andrea and I often went to English Bay to walk along the ocean and make sandcastles, even in the cold months. I would stand at the shore as I did as a child on Georgian Bay and breathe in the energy from the waves crashing on the shore. We loved to drive up Burnaby Mountain with a picnic to watch the hang-gliders sail off the cliffs. We did all these things alone, without Rick. He always had somewhere else to be.

I met Marg through a colleague of Rick's, and we hit it off right away. I was never good at making friends, and with moving so much, it was even more difficult. It felt good to have a girlfriend to talk to. We spent a lot of time together and formed a strong friendship, one that would last for decades. Life was the best it had been for a long while.

+++

Then Rick started drinking heavily again, coming home late or not at all. A few times, he would roll into bed late with cuts and bruises on his face and body, but it was always the other guy's fault for starting it. And the perfume, I could smell the perfume.

I began to wonder if Rick's never-ending loop of self-destruction would ever stop. What would I do if my marriage ended out there in the west, and I was without my family for support? I tried to push those thoughts away, but it was getting harder to do that every day. As I struggled to face reality, I knew one thing for sure: I needed to find a job to support Andrea and me. I applied for a loan officer position at CIBC and got the job. I had no experience in the banking field, but they were willing to train me, and I was willing to learn. I hired an after-school sitter for Andrea and went to work. The first week turned out to be a watershed moment for me.

I was being trained for the loan officer position by working alongside an experienced lender in downtown Vancouver. After a couple of days, I was ready to handle my first customer, who was an Indigenous man looking for a car loan. My trainer sat in the room to observe as I began taking the man's application. I could see my colleague becoming agitated as I completed the application and advised the man I would contact him the next day with the bank's decision. As soon as we were alone in the office, the senior loan officer turned to me and said, "That was a complete waste of time. We don't make Indians!"

I sat open-mouthed as he explained that it was bank talk for "we don't lend money to Indians." I felt sorry for the poor man who had given me his information in good faith. He seemed like a nice person, and I was confused and embarrassed for him. I thought about Britt and how my relatives were so ashamed of our roots. This was my first experience in the real world with blatant racism toward Indigenous people. I was uncomfortable.

"But he has a job and if everything else checks out, why would we turn him down?" I insisted.

"It doesn't matter," he said. "We don't lend to those people."

"Those people?" I repeated a little louder. "Even if they qualify for the loan?"

"Nope, no Indians on the books."

"I didn't see that in the training manual you gave me," I said, my face feeling hot.

"It's just something we all know," he replied, and then changed the subject.

Up to that point in my life, it never occurred to me to challenge this behaviour. I had been conditioned from a young child not to speak of my heritage. But as an adult, faced with such blatant evidence of racism, the force of it hit me hard. Until then, prejudices were always blurred with vagueness or denials. There it was, right in front of me — an unspoken rule about Indians.

I have never forgiven myself for not speaking up against what I believed was wrong, for not saying more. I wanted to tell him that I was one of "those people" and that part of me was Ojibwe. I wanted to defend the man who applied for the loan and push back on the unspoken rule. But it was my first day on the job, and sadly I was silent. I said nothing because that's what I'd been taught to do.

That incident stayed with me and would mark the moment when I began to consciously accept my Indigenous roots as part of me, part of who I am. The nagging guilt I felt just wouldn't go away. What if it had been my dad or one of my uncles? Would I have said something then? The fact that I was blond and passed for white made my silence worse, and my shame deepened. Soon after, I slowly began to open up to people about my heritage. I began by saying I was part Ojibwe, which was all I knew at the time. I wished my dad were still alive because I was finally ready to push for the answers I never learned as a child.

Other than that incident during my first week, I found the loan officer training easy and really enjoyed the job. I was assigned to the Lougheed Mall branch in Burnaby, just a few minutes from home. My salary was only $13,000 per year, but it would be enough for Andrea and me. It felt good to meet new people and have somewhere to go every day. And yes, I approved loans for people of every nationality if they qualified, including Indigenous applicants. I suspected that the bank's unwritten rules the person training me referred to were more about his prejudice than bank policy.

+++

One night around midnight, Rick came home with two guys from work. I gasped when I saw his white dress shirt covered in blood and bandages on half of his face and neck. He said that he was filled with morphine and had to go to bed and that the guys would explain. Then he left me standing there speechless with them while he went upstairs. The thing is, when I looked at him at that moment, I felt shocked at his appearance, but nothing inside of me moved. Usually when he was hurt, I hurt for his injuries, too, and would feel a sickness growing in my stomach to see him like that. It would knock the wind out of me. But this time, I had nothing left to feel except curiosity about what happened, and I simply watched him walk away. I felt no sadness, no concern, and no love. I was empty of all emotion when his friends told me the story.

Apparently, he was in a bar when he got into an altercation with another heavy-drinking patron. After a shouting match ensued, the guy broke the bottom off a beer bottle and jammed the jagged edges into Rick's face. The doctors had sewn him up with dozens of stitches along one side of his face, from his eye to his neck. When they finished, I simply asked if they wanted a drink, and we sat and talked about everything but Rick. I can't imagine what his friends thought of my cold reaction to Rick's injuries that night. But for me, despite feeling dead inside, it was a strange awakening.

I used my connections with lawyers at the bank to get some free legal advice about filing for divorce and custody rules. I knew Rick loved our daughter and would want to see her, but I wasn't about to give him joint custody. My lawyer assured me that with Rick's track record, he would get visitation rights at most.

One Saturday morning, when I returned from taking Andrea to ballet class, Rick was sitting in the living room with a fire on, drinking a coffee. He was hungover again and unshaven. The bandages were off his face, but the scar was an angry red slash across his cheek and neck. Kris Kristofferson was singing "Sunday Mornin' Comin' Down" on the stereo. I remember the conversation as if it were yesterday.

He caught me looking at him and said, "What?"

"Nothing," I replied, looking away.

"C'mon, spit it out. You want to say something. I know you do."

"I want a divorce," I blurted out.

He stared at me for a moment, and then he said, "What took you so long?"

To this day, I don't know why Rick didn't pull the plug on our marriage himself. After following him, believing in him, loving him, and waiting for him to want me again — that's all he could say. He didn't fight for us, ask me to stay, or tell me he loved me. Just "What took you so long?" Did he say this because he didn't care? Or was it because he didn't think he was worthy of keeping us? Either way, we had finally reached the end of a winding and treacherous road. While his question surprised me, I felt an overpowering sense of relief, like a bag of boulders had been lifted off my shoulders.

For ten years, I tried my best "to rise above it," as my mom said so often to us growing up. Maybe that's good advice in some situations, but now I needed to "rise up" instead and take control of my life. I'd been taught from an early age that fighting and causing a scene was never a good option. However, a decade of avoiding confrontation and staying silent hadn't worked for me. I needed to find a better way and show Andrea (and myself) this was not okay.

CHAPTER 11

Black Holes and Surprises

Rick moved out and rented an apartment in Vancouver. He had temporary visitation rights while we processed the divorce, and he saw Andrea every other weekend. A few months later, he called to tell me he'd been fired from Creditel and was moving back to Toronto.

Rick pushed to have our divorce fast-tracked, and I couldn't understand why it was so important to rush it. Turns out he was getting married again — to Jocelyn, the woman who had given him the picture and love note I'd found in my tea towel drawer at York University. I guessed it had been going on for a while. He got the decree absolute quickly and was married not long after that. Even though I wanted him gone, I felt cast aside and betrayed. On his wedding day, I made a little bonfire in my backyard. Into the firepit went my wedding dress, my veil, the white satin guest book from our reception, and a pile of invitation RSVPs. We didn't have a wedding album because Rick never paid the photographer, or I would have burned that too.

+++

I got things underway to sell the house and move back to Ontario. British Columbia was the most beautiful place I'd ever lived, and I could see myself making a good life there with my daughter. I loved the majesty of the ocean and the feelings of joyful renewal I always got from the crashing waves on the shore. But I missed my mom and siblings so much, and I didn't want Andrea to grow up without her family, and as sad as it was, she needed her father. She missed him even though he'd only been a part-time father. It was all she knew. Andrea saw the fun-loving dad who made her laugh and cuddled on the sofa with her singing Neil Diamond songs. It was time to get ready to go home.

+++

My first surprise came when the realtor I'd chosen to sell my house knocked on my door one evening looking embarrassed. He told me that he couldn't list the house. He said he did a title search and found out it was three months behind in mortgage payments, and the bank had foreclosed on the property.

"That's impossible," I told him. "Rick said he prepaid the mortgage for three months before heading back to Ontario." But he lied, and when I investigated, the house was indeed in foreclosure. The next surprise was getting a call from the Royal Bank, who advised me they were in the process of garnishing my wages at CIBC for back payments on a twenty-thousand-dollar loan I'd co-signed with Rick — which I never did. That's how my husband had obtained the down payment to buy the house. He forged my signature because I was with my mom in Ontario when he applied for the loan. I also found out my little green Monza was bought on credit, and I agreed to continue making the payments to keep the car.

I hired a lawyer to help me navigate through my financial woes, and he got a handwriting expert to release me from the Royal Bank debt. He also told me the best thing to do about my mortgage arrears was to walk away from the house in a "quit sale" when I was ready to leave. He said the bank would probably let me stay there for about a year.

At that time, the only person in my family who knew what I was going through was Estelle. We spoke at every opportunity, and I felt grateful to have her to talk to. She was still my best friend: supportive, non-judgemental, and encouraging. My sister was my rock. It took me a month to tell my mother that I'd asked Rick for a divorce and that he'd moved out. I'm not sure why I waited so long, but I was nervous about what she would say, despite her previous urgings for me to leave him and stay in Sudbury. Mom was very quiet on the phone when I told her he was gone. Then she shocked me by saying, "Why would you do that? Somebody is better than nobody."

I don't know exactly what response I was expecting from her, but it wasn't that one. Mom was always a resourceful, independent woman, who took control easily. I hoped she'd be proud of the decision I'd finally made. I had hidden many of Rick's dramas from her, but she knew him enough to understand how disastrous my marriage had been.

I've thought a lot about that statement over the years. It shook my confidence and hurt me at the time, but I believe she said those things out of love for Andrea and me. I'm certain it came from a place of fear, and it frightened her to think of the two of us alone thousands of miles away. Perhaps after Dad died, Mom found being on her own so frightening and painful that she didn't want that fate for me. Something had broken down the resilience and resolve I had witnessed my whole life. Mom was always the powerhouse in the family. But in that moment, she sounded like a weaker version of herself. Due to the long-distance phone charges, we talked only every couple of weeks. I was so self-absorbed in my own world of turmoil I hadn't noticed a change happening in her. I did everything I could to reassure her I was doing the right thing and would be home as soon as I could.

✦✦✦

It was around that time I started getting obscene phone calls at night. I thought the caller might be watching my house because he always called when I was alone or just after someone left. It was from the same male caller who disguised his voice and referred to me as "Trish," which is short for Patricia. I thought it might be someone who knew me. I felt afraid of being in the house alone with my young daughter, so I developed my own alarm system. I piled pop bottles and cans against the doors at night so that I would hear the commotion if someone broke in. I had Andrea sleep with me, and I kept the fireplace poker beside my bed.

One night when he called, the sound of his voice suddenly triggered a mental picture of a man I'd met at the bank. I thought it might be William, an usher at the theatre in the mall where I worked at CIBC. I'd given him a loan to buy a car, and he came in often to say hello. He was a shy, sloppy-looking young man in his early twenties with bad acne. I was surprised that he might be the guy. I felt rather sorry for him and always made time to say hello when he came into the bank.

I was alone with my five-year-old daughter and had to trust my instincts. I needed to protect her, to protect us both. The next day, with a shaky hand and wet armpits, I phoned him to ask if he'd meet me in the mall for a coffee. He sounded a bit flustered at getting my invitation and accepted.

I headed out to the coffee shop early to get there first. My heart was thumping hard enough to crack a rib. By the time he arrived, my hands were sweaty, and I could barely breathe. His hair was slicked back and still damp. He was wearing bell-bottoms and a paisley scarf tucked into the front of his shirt. Not exactly an ascot, but close enough to make me remember my mother's warning to "never trust a man who wears an ascot."

I wasted no time and got straight to the point. "William, are you making obscene phone calls to me?" My knees were in a nervous twitch under the table.

He was quiet and looked down, picking at a scab on his hands. "Well, the way I see it, I can't win," he said. "If I say yes, then you'll never talk to me again. If I say no, and the calls stop, you'll think it was me anyway."

When I saw the red crawling up his neck and heard the quiver in his voice, I was certain of my suspicions. "If you ever phone me again, William, I'll call the police. Shame on you!" I left him sitting there and walked back to my office with my stomach in my platform shoes. That was the end of my obscene calls.

William's car loan went into arrears the next month, and when I tried to contact him at the theatre, they told me he had quit his job and no one knew where he went.

That was my first lesson in finding my own way, and I felt the power that came from my actions. I'd stood up all alone, faced my obscene caller, and saved Andrea and me from a life of piling pop bottles against the door. I was not going to let this man make me feel small and afraid. It was a victory of epic proportions for the little girl from Britt.

◆◆◆

I sold everything I could to raise money for the moving expenses, including all my appliances. I even sold the built-in dishwasher, which I guess wasn't legally mine. I put the rest of Rick's clothes and shoes in a yard sale along with some furniture and household items not worth moving. Then, when Andrea finished her kindergarten year, I arranged for her to fly home to Rick and his new wife. I would finish things up at the house and then drive back to Ontario because I couldn't afford to ship my car. By that time, we'd been in British Columbia for only two years, but it seemed like a lifetime.

So in July 1977, when Andrea was six years old, I put her on a plane to go home, accompanied by an Air Canada stewardess. A couple of weeks later in August, I walked out of my empty house and checked into a hotel for my last night in British Columbia. I was sorry to leave my dear friend Marg and my neighbours, the RCMP officer, Jim, and his family.

Before I left, Jim gave me stern advice about being on the road alone: never stop to rest in a secluded spot, stop driving before dark, and keep my long hair tucked up into a hat when I'm in the car and in public. I was lonely, scared, and excited all at the same time.

I got in my Monza the next morning with my luggage in the trunk and my favourite brass lamp in the back seat. Glancing one last time at my carefully planned CAA TripTik, I put it down on the passenger seat beside me. Then, I got lost in the hotel parking lot looking for the exit. First, I burst into laughter and then broke down in tears. How would I ever find my way to Ontario?

With only eighteen months' driving experience, I put my car in gear and hoped for the best. I eventually found the exit and headed out of the hotel parking lot to find the Trans-Canada Highway.

+++

I woke up from my ten-year marriage to Rick with a lot of black holes in my memory — perhaps holes with deep secrets buried in the abyss. After we were divorced, his mother would recount certain events I had no memory of at all. She asked me once if I remembered when she found me crying outside their house in Levack. I was pregnant with Andrea and sitting on a snowbank in my nightgown with curlers in my hair. She said I'd never told her what happened to make me do that. I had no idea what she was talking about. I think about those black holes as a reflection of my state of mind. I was often depressed, overwhelmed, and without the skills to cope. As these blanks in my memory occurred over the years, I've never sought out professional help. Forgetting was my safe house.

Estelle once called me after she moved to Ottawa and made friends with people Rick and I had known there. She said, "I didn't know you were a bridesmaid at Dan and Lorrain's wedding." I said, "I wasn't." She insisted and said she saw Rick and me in their wedding album. I wouldn't believe her until she had Lorrain send me a picture, and there I was, smiling at the camera in a lovely aqua blue bridesmaid dress. This type of thing happened repeatedly over the years, and I've come to accept it.

Remembering the details of my life with Rick is like unpacking a trunk of sharp objects. I have to be careful not to cut myself all over again. I know there are probably other secrets lurking in the darkness, but I have no desire to shadow box my memories and remember any more than I have. I'm satisfied to keep the rest buried. I've forgiven Rick for all his indiscretions, and looking back, I know he had his internal monsters to battle, and they became his main focus. I understand him better now than I did then, and I feel compassion for him and nothing else.

Do I regret knowing this man or having married him? Not for one minute. I had a lot of growing up to do when I met Rick, and growing up is what I did. He took me on some pretty wild rides, but through it all, I became independent and more confident in my ability to survive. How else could I have confronted my obscene caller without being the person I had become? I'd finally learned that not speaking up for myself gives all the power to the other person. And being silent in my marriage to Rick had minimized my worth as a woman and as a mother to my daughter. I didn't want a life like that for her.

I loved Rick with a wilful abandon I would never feel again, and I chose to look away from his behaviour just to stay with him. Perhaps in telling myself he would change in time, what I was really hoping for was that I would change in time. It was always my choice to stay. I wasn't forced into anything. At first, I could forgive him for hurting me because he'd made mistakes. As he continued to hurt me, I realized it had become an unbroken pattern, which was harder to accept. But I did because it was the easiest thing to do. After growing up in a non-confrontational environment at home, that seemed like the natural option to me at the time. I had no idea how to fight for my rights.

I know in my heart Rick loved Andrea and me as much as he was capable of doing. But the lure of his demons and addictions was stronger and more compelling than the love he had for us. Still, he made me laugh, he made me cry, and dealing with him made me strong.

I realize it was more than love that kept me with him. It was a lack of imagination about my own future. I'd always thought of myself as part of a unit, first with my family, then with Rick. It was hard for me to think of myself as a person of my own making who could choose the life I wanted to live. As basic as that sounds today, I had no idea how to think that way. I'd never been taught how to dream about such things.

It took ten years of following Rick through the twisted branches of his life for me to learn to rely on myself — to see a glimmer of hope about my own future.

I pushed myself well beyond my comfort zone by setting out on a drive across Canada to start again as a single mother, something I couldn't have imagined myself doing when I arrived in British Columbia. I have the experience of living through the relationship dynamics with Rick to thank for all of that. But best of all, I got Andrea out of the deal! I'd do it all again just to have my beloved daughter in my life. I can't imagine my world without her.

Part Three (1977–1998)

A woman is like a teabag. You never know how strong it is until it's in hot water.

— Eleanor Roosevelt

CHAPTER 12

Bold Moves

As I drove along the Trans-Canada Highway, I felt a sense of accomplishment after my harrowing white-knuckle drive through Rogers Pass, a high mountain crossing in the Selkirk Mountains. As an inexperienced driver, if I had known ahead of time what a challenge that would be, with its steep winding roadways, dark narrow tunnels, and lack of any off-ramps, I might never have set out.

In many sections, there was a steep drop-off on the shoulder of the road, with a rock wall on the other side. I gripped the wheel and leaned forward in my seat as a mountain goat appeared out of nowhere. I slammed on the brakes, thankful I wasn't going fast. I prayed the driver in the car behind me was alert, and I worried I'd never make it home.

Following that challenging section of roadway, a couple of hours later I drove through Kicking Horse Pass in the Rockies, the highest point on the Trans-Canada Highway. The summer traffic was heavy, and the lanes in both directions were jammed with trailers and campers. The scenery was breathtaking with a blue haze of majestic mountains towering around me. Bald eagles soared through the deep gorges on the sides of the highway, and mountain goats were perched on the rocky ledges above the road. It was difficult to enjoy the scenery with my hands clamped on the steering wheel, sticky with tension.

It was an emotional time for me, all alone in my car, and I had a lot of time to think. I was making the long drive back to Ontario toward an unknown future, yet I began to feel giddy with excitement. I felt proud of myself for taking the leap, sweaty hands and all. But there was something else … I was feeling the joy of freedom for the first time since I was a child growing up in Britt. Surrounded by the majesty of the Rockies, it was a powerful and overwhelming realization. In later years, that drive through the mountains became my symbol of a breakthrough. It was like emerging from the depths of a deep sleep and realizing there was more to me than who I'd been. I don't know what triggered my big aha moment: the mountains, the solitude, the dizzying heights, or the fact that I'd shed one hundred and eighty pounds of husband. All I knew was that I'd finally made it through to the other side and I was ready to start again. It was a pivotal point in time and explains why thirty-two would become the age I'd forever see myself in dreams.

+++

As I made the trip across the western provinces, singing along with the Bee Gees, Neil Diamond, and Chicago, I began to relax and enjoy the ride. The fact that I was a thirty-two-year-old single mother with no home, no job, and no money didn't weigh me down. Yes, I was starting over yet again, but not because I was trailing behind my husband. This time, it was my choice, and I had a feeling of exhilaration. I trusted my little green car would help me find my way safely across Canada to a new life.

Other than the treacherous mountain passes, the rest of the trip went without incident. At the end of each day, I felt happy and exhausted, and fell into my bed at a roadside motel, some nights too tired to eat dinner. I remember belting out John Denver's "Take Me Home, Country Roads" when I passed from Manitoba into Northern Ontario.

+++

I arrived at my mother's house in Britt on the fifth day after leaving Vancouver. I didn't tell Mom I was driving home and just showed up at her door. I knew she'd worry about me being on the road alone. I saw her in the window as I parked my car, and I could tell she didn't recognize me. Mom had never seen my car, and I was wearing sunglasses with my hat pulled low on my forehead.

When I walked in the door, she sank into the nearest kitchen chair, then jumped up and crushed me in a hug. My mom rarely hugged, so this was a big deal. She said I was all skin and bones, and she was worried about the dark circles under my eyes. I was exhausted from the trip and welcomed her home cooking and hot rye toddies before bed. My ex-mother-in-law, Gert, would drive Andrea to Britt the next day, and I couldn't wait to see my baby. I'd made it home to my little house in Britt on the Magnetawan River, where I could recharge and soften everything I'd been through. It was where I needed to be: back at the beginning to start again.

+++

I spent the next week reuniting with my family and hugging the heck out of my daughter. I began to make plans for our future, where to live and where to look for a job. I decided Toronto would have the best opportunities, but Mom tried hard to convince me, once again, to live in Sudbury, where she and my siblings would be. Mom wanted to keep me close by and safe, and I loved her for it.

Despite all the bad things that went on in Sudbury when I lived there with Rick, I still loved the city. By that time, Sudbury had amalgamated, and the population had grown to almost 170 000. The people were warm and friendly; Andrea and I could make a good life there. It was an alluring option, where we would be protected and secure. But following Rick around had taught me that big cities like Vancouver and Toronto weren't nearly as scary as I'd imagined them to be. As a matter of fact, I found the busy hustle of city life exciting, and I felt larger and more relevant when I was there. Suddenly, things felt small for me when I thought of staying in Northern Ontario. For the first time, I was thinking longer term, and I wanted more. Mom couldn't understand my rationale but tried hard to support my decision.

I arranged to stay with an old friend in Toronto while I searched for work. Thankfully, CIBC hired me again, this time as a loan officer at Bayview Village, a high-end mall in the North York area of Toronto. I found the perfect townhouse right across the street and hoped they would have a vacancy. Clearly, the superintendent who interviewed me for the lease felt sorry for the mother and child standing in front of him looking for a home. He didn't do a credit check, which would have revealed my mortgage foreclosure in Vancouver. He put me at the top of a waiting list, and we got a unit right away. Andrea started grade one at a school down the street, and I went to work at CIBC in the mall. It was the perfect set-up, and for the first time, I could imagine a quiet, drama-free life with my daughter.

About a month after settling in, I was invited to attend a loan officer's seminar on lending. My boss said it would be a good opportunity for me to meet other people in my field, and I eagerly accepted. On the first day before the session started, I was outside the conference room talking on a pay telephone with a friend. Suddenly, I looked up, and my heart took a leap. "You should see the guy who just walked in! I didn't think CIBC had men who looked like that," I told her. I don't think he heard me, but he caught my eye and winked as he passed by.

His name was Bob Skene, and he was the main speaker at the conference. He worked as a senior lender for my region and was greeted by the audience with enthusiasm. The loan officers crowded around him to say hello, and I noticed him glance over to where I was sitting. He was an excellent speaker, with a good knowledge of the loan business and charisma to spare. With his sense of humour and quick thinking, he easily managed the crowd, answered challenging questions, and always got his point across with professionalism. Bob was an imposing six-foot-four replica of Tom Selleck, complete with a self-possessed confidence, black moustache, hazel eyes, and dimples. I estimated he was about ten years older than I was, in his early forties.

On the afternoon break, I got up my nerve to approach him. I introduced myself, and he held me in his gaze while we talked about the loan business and my move from British Columbia. He had done some fishing in the Britt area, and we talked about that too. He spent the entire break time with me while other attendees impatiently lined up to get his attention. I noticed he wasn't wearing a ring, so before we returned to our seats, I took a deep breath and did a bold thing. I said, "Do you date loan officers?"

He looked at me with a twinkle in his eye and flashed those dimples. "I do now," he said.

"Then have dinner with me," I answered with my biggest smile.

+++

I'll never forget our first date. We met at the Toronto Squash Club for drinks before going to dinner. I found him charming and interesting, and there was definitely a sexual chemistry between us. When we left to head out to the restaurant, he stopped on the sidewalk outside the club. He was incredibly handsome in his dark suit and long Burberry trench coat. I was wearing four-inch stilettos, and he still towered over me. Bob faced me, held both my shoulders, looked at me with those incredible hazel eyes, and said, "You know, we've never kissed, and I'll never know when to make the right move. So, if we kiss now, we'll get it over with, and then we can relax and go to dinner. Okay?"

I was impressed with his unique approach, but he already had me with the dimples and trench coat. We had our first kiss right there on busy Lombard Street.

I'd never slept with a man on a first date, but I made an exception with Bob Skene. He followed me home in his car after dinner, and as soon as I dismissed the babysitter, we went to bed as naturally as if I'd known him for years. Sex with him was like an explosion and unlike anything I'd felt in my limited experience. Before I could quietly get him out of my place in the morning, Andrea came out of her bedroom and met him in the hall carrying his shoes.

"Who are you?" she asked him. I quickly explained he was a friend as she looked up at his towering height. Bob had played football for twenty years and was still built like a linebacker. After all the times I'd shielded her from meeting the few men I dated, here I was caught with a towering giant of a man coming out of my bedroom.

Bob had been married for ten years before he was divorced. He had no children but spent time with his young niece, so he seemed comfortable enough with Andrea and handled the situation well. She showed him her room, and he helped her untangle the strings of a puppet her dad had given her. She didn't have any questions when he left, so I think the meeting traumatized me more than my daughter.

Just before I met Bob, he'd purchased a house in the Beach area of Toronto. It was a fixer-upper, and he was busy doing a lot of the renovations himself. For the first year we dated, he went between the makeshift rooms at his house and my place. Bob, Andrea, and I got closer over that year, and I remember one incident that cemented my belief that he would make a great stepdad for my daughter.

One night after dinner, when Andrea was about seven years old, she went to the little playground right outside my living room window to play on the swings. A few minutes later, she came crying into the house. She said someone had written a bad word about her on the cement. Bob took her by the hand and asked her to show him. Some kid had written "Andrea is a f***" in chalk.

As calm as could be, they returned to the house, where Bob filled a bucket with soap and water and took her by the hand back to the playground. He got down on his hands and knees and scrubbed every word off the cement. When they returned, Andrea's bare feet were filthy with mud, but she was smiling from ear to ear. As I prepared to give her a bath, Bob picked her up, flipped her upside down, and, holding her above his head, told her to put her footprints on the ceiling. Those footprints were still there when I left the townhouse a year later.

CHAPTER 13

A Good Man

Once Mom adjusted to life without Dad, she seemed happy and more lighthearted. She loved to tease and could be quite a prankster. This was a playful side of her I didn't see very often when we were children and she was laden with responsibilities.

Estelle and I shared all our secrets, so she knew about Bob. I hadn't yet told my mother, but she suspected I was seeing someone because she told me she read it in her cards. One day, Mom and Aunt Bernice arrived in Toronto to stay with me for a couple of days. Bob was away on a business trip, so the timing was perfect. Before giving them my bedroom, I removed anything in the closet that belonged to Bob and took his shaving products out of the bathroom. They were unpacking their things when they both came down the stairs giggling like two schoolgirls.

"And just who do these belong to?" my mom said, grinning like a Cheshire cat. She was holding a pair of Bob's size thirteen shoes, which I had missed under the bed. With a red face, I told them about Bob, and they made me promise to bring him to Britt so that they could meet the man who belonged to those big feet.

A couple of weekends later, we arrived at Mom's house. I told Bob I had no idea what she would do about the sleeping arrangements, but he was cool with anything. Mom was very gracious when she met Bob and surprised us when she said, "I can't let you sleep together under my roof, but you can take the front cabin. What you do there is your own business." She had a mischievous look on her face, and I think she enjoyed watching us squirm. After the weekend, she took me aside and said, "I like him. He's a good man." I knew Bob was a good man from the way he treated my daughter and me. He was always respectful and loving, and I could count on him for keeping his word. That simple validation from my mother made me happy.

✦✦✦

My job at CIBC was going well, and I worked hard to learn everything I could. The bank was awarding an all-expenses-paid trip to its high performers across the country. I was among the loan officers who won a trip for two to England. My mom was the first person I called to announce my exciting news.

"Why on earth would you want to go there?" she asked me. "You'll have to fly over the ocean." Poor Mom was still trying to keep me under that wing of hers. Her reaction didn't dampen my enthusiasm, and I invited Bob to come with me.

We had a glorious time, staying in a beautiful hotel in downtown London, with all excursions and dinners arranged for us for the entire week. Every minute was so exciting I didn't want to go to sleep. Bob and I took vacation time and went to Paris for a few days before coming home. We booked a room at the Odeon Hotel, a romantic little place in the Latin Quarter. We walked around the city, climbed the Eiffel Tower, and ate frogs' legs at Roger La Grenouille. Bob was a more experienced traveller, but this was my first trip overseas, and I was hooked.

⁂

In December of the same year, my mother was ready to carry out her plans to live in Sudbury. She sold her house in Britt to two of my cousins and stayed with Estelle and John while she looked for a place. They lived just outside of Sudbury, and she'd been spending her winters with them since Dad died. Mom had been having some health problems, so her doctor admitted her to the Sudbury General Hospital for bladder surgery. She called me from her hospital room and sounded fine, just a bit anxious about being there. Her operation would be the next day, and I said I would call her then. An hour later, my brother-in-law John called me. His voice was strained and quiet. "I'm sorry, Pat. Your mom had a stroke."

"That's impossible!" I told him. "I just got off the phone with her."

"Well, it must have happened afterwards," he said. "But thankfully, it wasn't too severe." I told him I would drive to Sudbury the next day.

In the middle of the night, John called again to tell me my mom had another stroke, a massive one this time, and Estelle said I should come right away.

Mom never recovered. She stayed in the hospital for the next five months and died the following May. It was a devastating loss to Bruce,

Estelle, Maureen, and me. She was only sixty-seven years old and had survived Dad by three years. Now the house in Britt was gone, both parents were gone, and I felt untethered, adrift in the world without an anchor.

Bob stuck to me like a second skin during that time of healing. He didn't coddle me; he simply helped me move forward by being loving, kind, and hilarious. That man could tell a joke like nobody I'd ever met. He had a wide circle of friends, and since I didn't bring much to the relationship in that department, his friends became my friends. We kept busy with an active social life, but when I missed my mom and dad and needed to be alone, he gave that to me as well. There was nothing like a good cuddle time with my daughter to put things back into perspective.

+++

With our parents gone, Bruce, Estelle, Maureen, and I vowed to stay close, despite living in separate cities. Maureen and her husband had a lovely cottage on the Magnetawan River in our hometown of Britt. It was a beautiful spot right at the mouth of Georgian Bay. That became our new meeting place. We started a "girls' week" where we three sisters left our husbands and kids behind every summer and got together to catch up with one another and have some fun. My sister-in-law, Ann, always joined us for a few days.

But first we'd start the week off with our annual Lamondin picnic, choosing a site on an island out in Georgian Bay. Shore dinners had always been a big part of our life, something that had gone on in our family for generations. It made sense that this became our way to connect.

Everyone in the family was included in the picnic part of our girls' week — our husbands, cousins, aunts, uncles, and all the kids. Bob had never experienced a family like mine, and he looked forward to this event as much as Andrea and I did every year. Sometimes, we had four generations there, all arriving in boats at one of the secluded islands. The location was chosen every year based on the day's weather conditions and how choppy the waters were in Georgian Bay.

My cousin Anne would bring her accordion, and Uncle Ernest and my cousin Wally brought their guitars. We sang songs, cooked fish on an open fire, drank pop and beer, ate sandwiches, and swam in the clear waters of the bay. There could be thirty or forty people there, whoever could make it that year.

Sometimes, my brother-in-law Dave would disappear into the trees and emerge dressed like Father Guido Sarducci from *Saturday Night Live*. We'd howl with laughter as he walked around and gave us his blessing. The picnic went on for hours until the sun sank into the horizon and the mosquitoes drove us back to Dave and Maureen's cottage. There, we crammed into the living room and continued singing for hours. We included contemporary songs, country and western, and always the classics for the older generation. Some of our favourites were "Four Strong Winds," "The Rose," "Amazing Grace," "You Are My Sunshine," "Goodnight Irene," and "Cruising Down the River." Several members of our family had beautiful singing voices and sang a few solos for the group.

I just took it for granted at the time, until I realized most people I knew didn't have these types of get-togethers. But to my Métis family, celebrations that included the sharing of food, music, and storytelling were as natural as breathing. The water and land bound us together as it had for our ancestors, and Georgian Bay was an important sense of place for our family. What I know now is that my Métis culture never disappeared. Even though I didn't know how to name it, I never stopped living Métis. It's always been with me.

The next day, everyone went home, leaving only the women and girls in the family. Girls' week became a tradition that would go on for thirty years. We eventually stopped having the picnics due to health issues and a shortage of boats, and with growing families, it was getting harder to accommodate everyone in town. But we still got together every summer at Dave and Maureen's cottage on a smaller scale.

✦✦✦

In 1979, when Bob finished most of the renovations on his house, he asked Andrea and me to move in with him. He'd grown up in the Beach area and said it was a great neighbourhood for raising kids. His mother lived a block away and could babysit for us when we went out. The truth was I was in love with this big hulk of a man. When I was with him, I felt like nothing in the world could ever hurt me again. Although he was very different from my dad, there was a quiet softness about Bob that reminded me of my father. Andrea was getting quite attached to him as well, so it was a good package deal. Thankfully, he wasn't a drinker, and that was a big plus in my books.

So, there I was again, in another relationship without taking a breather from the last one to be alone. But saying that, I felt more cautious and knew I was getting a good man, just as my mother had said. We'd been seeing each other for two years at that point, and neither one of us was in a rush to get married. Bob was still feeling the sting from his first marriage; his wife cheated on him with his best friend. And given my history with Rick, I was happy to live together and take Bob for a test run for a few years before making another life commitment.

A couple of months later when my townhouse lease was up, we moved into Bob's house on Neville Park Boulevard, in the Beach, a place where we would live for the next twenty-two years. It was still only partially finished because he was doing most of the work himself when he had the time. But it was good enough to move in. Some of the doors had no doorknobs and wouldn't have until we sold it two decades later. One year, Andrea asked for a doorknob for her bedroom for Christmas, which Santa was happy to provide.

Andrea had a hard time switching schools yet again. She had lived through so many moves and changes in her young life. My heart hurt to see her struggling to make new friends in a strange neighbourhood. She was starting grade three, and this would be her third school in four years. Sometimes, I'd leave work early and hide at the back gate peeking into the schoolyard at recess. I wanted to see if she was alone or playing with friends. Thankfully, she was always with one or two other girls.

We were not in the suburbs filled with young families and kids. We lived on an old, established street, with no children that I could see. I was determined to find a neighbourhood friend for my daughter. I told Bob I was taking Andrea out for a walk to see if I could find some children to introduce her to. When we came home an hour later with no results, he said, "Geez, Pat. Next time, why don't you tie a pork chop around her neck? That should at least attract a stray dog." The sexiest thing about this man was the way he made me laugh.

I can still see Bob at school plays, all six-foot-four of him, crawling up the aisle on his belly like a reptile to get the best shot of Andrea with his camera. Eventually, she adjusted, and we all settled into our new life together. We loved the Beach with its biking paths, beautiful boardwalk, eclectic selection of restaurants, and small-town community atmosphere. It was only twenty minutes from downtown Toronto.

+++

Bob and I worked hard at our careers. I was still a loan officer in a branch when the marketing rep for my area dropped in and asked me what my career plans were. I told him I wanted his job. He laughed and said I could never do that, but they had openings for lower clerical positions. I said no thanks; I'd wait for something better. A year later, I replaced him in marketing at CIBC's head office on Bay Street when they transferred him to a branch. He never said a word.

Bob left CIBC for a better position and became the Director of Mortgages for the Royal Bank, right nearby me in the Toronto-Dominion Centre. We had a short commute together, and things were going well. Bob was confident and outgoing and emboldened me to pursue my career and stand up to the men who stood in my way. "Be seen and be heard," he used to tell me. He demanded nothing from me, and I found the relationship easygoing and comfortable. But he still gave me butterflies when I saw him at the end of each day. Bob and Andrea were developing a strong relationship, and he was patient with her and knew how to calm her when she was upset.

My friend Marg, from British Columbia, transferred to Toronto with her company and was now living close by in the Beach. We spent a lot of time together, and I was delighted to have her back in my life again. She was a very attractive strawberry blond, who enjoyed a colourful and adventurous sex life. Her epic stories fascinated me and, at times, sent me into convulsions of laughter. We were so different, and I loved having her as a friend.

In 1982, after five years of test driving our relationship, Bob and I decided to get married. It was a small but elegant affair on New Year's Eve at Windows Restaurant, at the top of the Four Seasons Hotel in Toronto. Bob and I were so happy, surrounded by thirty-five of our close friends and family. I wrote a poem for my vows, and Bob made a beautiful ad-lib speech about his love for Andrea and me, and how we made the perfect package deal. It was a beautiful wedding and a magical New Year's Eve.

+++

We didn't go on a honeymoon, but we always travelled as much as we could, leaving Andrea with Bob's mother. My love for seeing the world grew with each trip we took. Many times, I thought of Mr. Powell and the world travels he introduced me to through his postcards and gifts. As soon as we were back home from one adventure, I started planning the next.

One year, we took a month-long vacation to Portugal and Spain. It was a long time away from Andrea, but she would be staying with Bob's mom again. I felt pangs of guilt about leaving her during our travels, but taking her out of school at such a young age wasn't an option. Bob and I were also working longer hours, and we missed many dinners and evenings with her. I could feel the heaviness in my heart when I thought about it, but I wanted to do well in my job and prove myself, so I ignored the feeling. I thought there would always be time to make up for my absence. Andrea became a latchkey kid and never complained about our absences. I was obsessed with my work and felt less and less guilt about leaving her. I told myself she was a good kid and managed just fine, between home, school, and at home with my mother-in-law.

My fortieth birthday fell on the weekend before we left for Portugal. Bob told me he had a surprise for me, and I shouldn't plan anything for Saturday night. He didn't offer any other details. On the big day, he made me stay in the bedroom with the radio on while he got things underway and then called me to come downstairs. My house was full of people! They were dressed like children; the women wore frilly dresses and pigtails, and some of the guys had on beanies with little air propellers on top. My friend Lynda had painted freckles on her nose, and her husband wore short pants and suspenders. I stood on the stairs and gawked at them. They all started singing "Happy First Kid's Birthday Party!"

Bob knew I'd never had a birthday party as a child and decided to give me one for my fortieth. We played pin the tail on the donkey, twirled hula hoops out on the deck, and had a scavenger hunt on the main floor. We ate barbecued hot dogs and hamburgers, potato chips, lollipops, and an incredible chocolate cake for dessert. It was stacked five layers high and encased in a ganache frosting with long thin triangles of chocolate standing on the top. One star-shaped sparkler stood tall in the centre of the cake.

That night, Bob gave me a beautiful porcupine quill box made by Ojibwe artisans from Manitoulin Island. I'd started collecting these boxes a few years before, and I loved the artistry: birchbark bases covered with designs made of porcupine quills and trimmed with sweetgrass. Bob beamed with joy when he saw how happy I was to receive such a special gift. Could I possibly love this man any more?

Bob was always proud of my Ojibwe roots, and while I was still holding back, he was never hesitant to tell our friends about my heritage. He suggested I self-identify even back then. But I was so far from knowing anything about my ancestors at that point I didn't know where to start. Something about these intricate quill boxes linked me to a past I knew so little about. I tried again and again asking my aunt Bernice about what she knew of our Ojibwe roots. She was the last remaining relative on my dad's side. Her eyes would get wide, and she'd shake her head. "There's no Ojibwe in our family" is all she would say.

I found myself drawn to the sweetgrass I grew up with as a child and kept sprigs of it in my home. I learned about smudging from an Indigenous woman at the Whetung Ojibwa Centre at Curve Lake First Nation. And I bought deerskin moccasins at the French River Trading Post every summer. I seemed to have an internal compass steering me toward these items. All I knew for sure was that they gave me a feeling of connection and comfort I couldn't explain.

+++

Rick was still in and out of Andrea's life, and she saw him regularly for a while, until he left Jocelyn for his third wife. That one didn't last more than a year when he married his fourth wife, who was the lawyer who handled his divorce from number three. Soon after that, he moved to Seattle with her, and they settled there. He didn't provide much in the way of child support over the years other than a few sporadic payments mostly made by Jocelyn when he was married to her.

Rick's idea of support was taking Andrea on a vacation to Grand Bahama or shopping in New York. When she was fourteen, he took her to Saks Fifth Avenue and bought her an Italian leather skirt and emerald earrings. I was fine with it. I couldn't afford those things and also pay for her braces, school supplies, and everyday needs. Andrea was impressed and happy, and that's all that mattered. Bob's idea of a great gift differed from Rick's. That same year, Bob gave her a small portfolio of blue chip stocks.

Bob's relationship with Andrea grew when she was in her teens. My teenage years had been sheltered, and I was naïve about the temptations and dangers of that age. But Bob certainly wasn't. He made a pact with her to call him anytime she was in an uncomfortable situation or felt like things were getting out of her control. He said he would come to get her, no questions asked. She took him up on that offer several times, and he'd jump out of bed into his track pants and take off in the car. He might have had a pact with her, but it didn't stop me from giving her the third degree the next day.

As good a dad as Bob was to Andrea and fun to be around, he had his dark sides too. He was often bull-headed and lost his temper at the smallest of things. He was far more social than I was and would fill our weekends with outings and events, which I often found exhausting. He had a few friends I didn't like, and we would argue when he wanted to spend more time with them than I did. But I was learning how to hold my ground and push back when I didn't want to do something. That was new for me. It was the eighties, and women were becoming more empowered. I'd read Gloria Steinem's book *Outrageous Acts and Everyday Rebellions*. I felt she was talking directly to me when she wrote about masculine expectations of the women in their lives. She made me want to make myself matter more, and I started practising what she was preaching in my own way.

CHAPTER 14

A Mighty Bag of Beans

I never considered myself a strong woman. There wasn't much left of the little spitfire who set the bushes aflame as a child. Or the scrappy kid sister who knocked the wind out of her brother with an old broom. Slowly, over time, that spunky little girl in me seemed to be replaced by some weaker doppelganger. Perhaps she was simply worn out from being worn down. She certainly wasn't anywhere to be found at Marymount or in my muted silence when I was married to Rick. I try to imagine how things would have been different in high school and in my marriage if I'd been more assertive, more confident in what I wanted. I was who I was then, and the path had been rough, but it also gave me strength.

Since leaving Vancouver and meeting Bob, I sometimes felt a hint of the old spunkiness returning. I was becoming more confident about standing up for myself at work and in my relationship. Bob was a big man who lived big and loved hard, and I enjoyed the ride with him. I was not athletic, but Bob taught me how to play squash and racquetball. I joined the Adelaide Club downtown to play with Marg on my lunch hour and after work. Marg always told me I had a killer instinct on the racquetball court. Bob taught me to be bold and to step out of my comfort zone: to try strange foods, to drive in unfamiliar areas of the city, and to travel with a map instead of a tour guide. He would tease and call me "One-Way Patsy" because I followed a set pattern to my routines. He'd tease me, saying, "That one-road town you came from runs deep."

Bob was at ease anywhere, and with him I began to overcome my discomfort of trying new things. We travelled every year but never with a tour group. We planned our own itinerary and found our way around by walking and using local transportation options. Many times, we didn't speak the language, but we always managed to muddle through. Travelling the world became a passion for us both.

When Bob walked into a room, people noticed. Certainly, his size had something to do with it, but he was a big presence wherever we went; I felt more confident in exploring the edges when I was with him. Bit by bit and through his support, I became brave. Bob supported me in a way that helped me to dig deep and find my voice. I was becoming a person who stands up for herself and what she believes in … which leads me to my "bag of beans" story.

✦✦✦

Since the Beach area was close to downtown Toronto, every Saturday morning around six o'clock, we would go to the St. Lawrence Market for our meat, fish, and fresh produce. We loved it there. The atmosphere was friendly, and Bob knew all the vendors by name. We always looked forward to enjoying the market's famous peameal bacon on a bun as our reward for getting up so early.

One Saturday, we had Estelle's fifteen-year-old daughter, Andi, staying with us. She was leaving to go home to Ottawa later that day, so we planned on going to the market before she had to board a plane at the Toronto Island Airport. When we arrived at the market with her at two in the afternoon, many vendors were starting to close their booths. We didn't like to go at this time of day because there were often seedy characters wandering through the place looking for handouts. But the market was quiet, and we split up to get the list done. Bob stayed upstairs for the meat and fish while Andi and I went downstairs for the vegetables.

I found a vendor closing shop and selling off green string beans. He offered to give me an enormous bag of them for two dollars. My niece stood a few feet off to the side as I reached across the counter to take the bag and give the man my money. Suddenly, I felt two hands reach around from behind and grab both my breasts. My first reaction was "Why would Bob do this in public?" But when I whipped around, I came face to face with a man grinning at me, my eyes locked on his baked-bean teeth. His hair hung in greasy strands around his face, and the stench of his stale breath in my face reeked of last night's bottle. I knew that smell well from my days with Rick.

I stood there like a mannequin, staring at him as he fondled my breasts again and then turned to walk away. My niece was frozen on the spot watching the whole thing, her eyes wide with panic. The man looked back at me with his watery bloodshot eyes and grinned defiantly, then headed for the door to leave. I watched him, my feet stuck to the floor, legs like rubber, as I desperately looked around for someone to help me. But there weren't many shoppers in the market, and it all happened so fast that no one except my niece witnessed my assault. The heat rose in my face, and my heart thundered in my ears. *You can't just let him walk away. He grabbed your breasts! He assaulted you!*

Something snapped, and I took off after him, swinging my bag of beans in wide circles like a Spanish bola. His back was to me, so he didn't see me coming. He was about to push the doors open to leave when my bag of beans made contact with his head. I beaned him on his right ear with every ounce of strength I had. He howled like a banshee and whipped around, screaming in my face.

"What the f*** ya do that fer, ya stupid b****?"

That's when I noticed he wasn't alone. He had a buddy with him, and I backed up as the two of them walked toward me with clenched fists. As the two thugs got closer, I considered making a run for it. In that split second, I knew all one hundred and ten pounds of me couldn't fight them physically, so all I could hope for was insanity.

I dropped my bag of beans and stood my ground, both hands on my hips, facing them dead on as you would to scare away a wild animal in the bush. Then I went totally berserk and began to scream obscenities into their faces, as my whole body burned with rage. I waved my fists in the air and spit out one vile curse after another. I didn't budge an inch from my spot. The few people who were still in the lower level of the market gathered around to see what the commotion was all about.

Seeing this, the two thugs retreated and turned on their heels to leave the building, calling me a vulgar name for female genitalia. When it was all over, I glanced at my niece, who was standing motionless with her hands over her mouth, looking like she'd been turned to stone. I flopped onto a bench still trembling, and she sat beside me looking terrified. My heart blasted a steady drumbeat in my ears. We looked at each other, our eyes still wide with shock, and burst out laughing. "I can't wait to tell your sister about this!" she said.

When I found my legs again, we went upstairs to meet Bob, and Andi breathlessly told him what happened. He was furious and wanted to chase the guy down, but I convinced him that he was long gone back to the streets. Then Bob said, “So, do you still have the beans?”

I had no idea who that inner scary witch was or where she was storing all that anger … and pure guts! I didn’t recognize myself, and although I was proud of not letting him just walk away, I was shocked by my behaviour. Where did all that fury and black rage come from? Was it pent up from years of feeling diminished and less than I was, or was it there simmering under the surface all the time? Was it the smell of alcohol that triggered a reminder of the years I had given up by putting up and shutting up? Something had definitely popped my cork.

I realized I needed to become more of that girl with guts, but the depth of my rage was frightening. I was not remorseful for my aggressive actions, only shaken by the event. I saw a side of myself that frightened and excited me at the same time. I realized then that I could fight back. I defended myself against a wrong that was being done to me. The incident kept me awake for several nights as I relived the moment. I felt something big had happened, and I was much stronger for it.

When my niece arrived home in Ottawa, Estelle had a house full of company. My sister told me she walked in the door and shouted, “Hold everything, people! Have I got a story for you!”

CHAPTER 15

Divine Intervention

Andrea was in her final year of high school when we noticed a lot of unexplained bruising on her arms. I had the doctor do some blood tests, and in the middle of studying for her grade thirteen exams, she was admitted on an urgent basis to Mount Sinai Hospital. Her platelet count was dangerously low; even a cough could make her bleed to death. She had a rare autoimmune blood condition called ITP (idiopathic thrombocytopenic purpura). The doctors explained they would need to do a spinal tap the next day.

"What are you looking for?" I asked. "Do you know what's wrong with her?"

"Her low platelet count could indicate leukemia, so we need to rule that out right away," he answered.

"Leukemia" was all I heard before my ears started to ring. I watched the doctor's mouth moving, but I couldn't hear any more words. I understood then why she was in the cancer ward of the hospital. I felt like my life ended at that moment when the doctors said the L word. I don't know how I made it home; I could barely see the road through my tears. The house was empty when I got there. Bob was still not aware of what had happened that day. He was at a business event, and I couldn't reach him. I paced the floor, crying and clutching at the pain in my chest. I had never faced such blackness.

I don't know if my mother channelled herself into my brain at that moment, but I suddenly remembered her telling me about the power of novenas. It's a sort of Catholic bargaining with God, where you pray for a specific intention for nine days and make a personal offering, similar to giving something up for Lent. Chocolate was always my favourite food, the most delicious of all the deliciousness in the world. I got down on my knees, and despite my disdain for the Catholic Church since leaving Marymount, I hoped God was still there for me. I promised Him that if He made Andrea well, I would give up chocolate, not for the nine-day novena devotion period, but for the rest of my life. I would never eat chocolate again. I prayed God would hear my prayer through the roaring in my head. When Bob got home, he found me sobbing in that position at the side of our bed. He held me tight to his chest and shared my pain as I blubbered through the details.

To our tremendous relief, the spinal tap was negative for leukemia or cancers of any kind, but the doctors could find no specific reason for Andrea's condition. They did keep her in the hospital for a couple of weeks and started her on high doses of prednisone to get her blood healthy again. I felt like a very old woman when we finally took her home.

She healed well and was back to normal in a couple of months. The school forgave the exams she missed because of her illness and averaged her yearly marks for university transcripts. That September, we moved her into an apartment in London, Ontario, where she would start first year at Western University. Since that day, I have never eaten chocolate.

✦✦✦

Bob and I missed Andrea terribly. We compensated by putting more hours into our careers, coming home late and exhausted. By that time, I'd fought my way through the male barricades in banking to reach the position of Vice President of Consumer Loans. Most women at my level were in traditionally female roles like marketing or human resources, while men generally occupied more technical positions like mine.

I remember some years earlier when the vice president job was posted. There would be a panel of six executive male interviewers selecting the candidate. I'd heard they preferred someone new from outside the bank, so it took months for a headhunter to find a list of suitable candidates from both Canada and the United States. Although I knew my chances were slim without educational credentials, I applied anyway, confident I could do the job. When I eventually got my one-hour interview with the panel, I was in my groove and thought I'd handled the questions well. I left feeling good, knowing I'd done my best whatever the decision. One of the interviewers ran down the hall after me and said, "Wow! Where have you been? What took you so long to get to this level?" And there it was again: "What took you so long?" Exactly the same words Rick had used when I told him I wanted a divorce.

I was already in my early forties at the time, and this guy was about thirty-three and already two levels above the job for which I was applying. He was from a prominent family on the west coast. While what he said was rather insulting, how would I begin to explain "what took me so long" to this good-looking, confident young man who had lived a life of privilege and opportunity and was now on the fast track to becoming chairman of the board? How could he ever understand my experience of growing up in a family who experienced shame and discrimination? What would he think of a childhood with outdoor toilets and a home with no electrical wiring? A life where higher education and opportunity were out of reach for most families? And a ten-year lifetime of living with an alcoholic? I simply gave him my corporate smile and said, "So my interview went well?"

My boss called me at home that night to tell me I'd gotten the vice president job. That moment will always be one of the biggest highlights in my life. The little girl from Britt had made the big time.

I travelled a lot on business, throughout Canada and the United States, and I made a few overseas trips. Bob also did some travelling for his work, and more and more, we seemed to be leading separate lives.

Bob and I were becoming more distant and spent more time with our own activities than with each other. We'd been together for about fifteen years, and as wonderful as Bob was, he wasn't perfect, and neither was I. He could be stubborn and had a terrible habit of pouting when he didn't get his way. Once, when I cut my long hair into a shoulder-length bob, he didn't speak to me for three days. More and more, we played racquetball and squash at our own clubs with other people instead of each other. He sometimes lost his temper at the smallest of things, like a car cutting into traffic, someone talking in a movie, or his Sunday morning eggs being too hard-boiled. As much as I loved him, I found his reaction to these types of things upsetting, and our growing distance didn't help.

I suspected Bob might be seeing someone, but I had no proof. He'd always asked my opinion about work matters because we were both in the banking business. But he stopped discussing his job and barely listened when I talked about mine. He simply looked unhappy when he was at home and seemed uninterested in me. A lot of the time I felt the same way about him. Our sex life was stalled, and I wondered if I was heading into another sexless marriage. I was a hair's breadth away from having an affair. I'd always had a lot of attention from men; I was in a man's environment after all. No one ever came close to what I had at home, and I'd never before considered cheating on Bob. But I met a man who was different. I found him exciting to be with, and it was exhilarating to feel the thrill of a new relationship, that sense of passion again. It also felt wrong, and I hated myself for even thinking about it. But nothing had happened yet, and deep down, I didn't want to be that woman.

While this was going on, we were invited to join our friends John and Lynda on a sailing trip to the Grenadine Islands in the Caribbean. The four of us did a lot of travelling together, and several years prior, we'd all enjoyed a month-long trip to China, Japan, Korea, Hong Kong, Macau, and Thailand. I was hopeful the time away would give Bob and me a new environment to help us relax and find each other again.

+++

We rented a forty-two-foot sailboat in St. Vincent for a week and hired a local captain to help us navigate. We'd all done some sailing, with John the most experienced of the four, but not enough to handle the wild waters of the Grenadine Islands.

We boarded the beautiful boat and set sail. Everything went well for the first few days. We lived in our bathing suits, dropped anchor to enjoy the white sands of Macaroni Beach at Mustique, swam ashore to visit a local bar at Petit St. Vincent, and gagged on a dinner of sea turtle at Salt Whistle Bay. Other than the occasional bout of seasickness for Bob and me, we were doing well enough. But occasionally, he still managed to say something to upset me. Like the day I asked him if he liked my new yellow bathing suit and he said, "Women over forty shouldn't wear bikinis." Insulting my appearance was a first for Bob, and I was embarrassed in front of John and Lynda. His remark hurt me, but it was easier to laugh it off and make a joke of it.

+++

I loved to snorkel. I first learned how to do it on a trip to Hawaii with Bob several years before. He had experience in both snorkelling and scuba diving and had been enthusiastic to teach me. Putting my head underwater and telling myself to breathe through the snorkel was no easy thing to master. But when I finally got the hang of it, I enjoyed the magical underwater show of hundreds of exotic fish, a rainbow of coral reefs, and an array of bizarre creatures of the sea. It was like exploring an unknown world.

I'd been snorkelling on vacations with Bob several times since then. So, when John suggested we anchor and jump off the sailboat to snorkel, I thought it was a great idea. But this time, we were in the wild waters of the Caribbean and keeping afloat in the churn of the waves was tiring. I'd never snorkelled with a life jacket on and wasn't wearing one then. I quickly became winded and frankly, out there in the middle of the ocean, I was afraid of meeting a shark. Lynda was snorkelling while lying on an air mattress because she wasn't a strong swimmer, so she was fine. And the two guys had taken off toward the reef. I returned to the boat after about fifteen minutes. Instead of being helpful or protective of me as he had been in the past, Bob became annoyed when he saw me out of the water. He pulled off his mask and yelled, "What the hell's wrong with you?" When I answered that I was tired, he rolled his eyes, put his mask back on, and went back to join John.

I sat in the boat alone while the others were in the water. I began thinking about a trip we took to Belize a few years before, where we rented a small skiff and snorkelled alone at the barrier reef, the second largest coral reef in the world. It was an amazing experience with loads of exotic sea life and even a few moray eels glaring back at us from below. At one point, I left Bob in the water and climbed back in the boat to clean my mask and put on more sunblock. While I was sitting there, a dark shadow passed by me under the water. It was a ten-foot nurse shark! Bob had no idea it was there, so I jumped back into the water to warn him of the danger. Thankfully, we both made it safely back into the skiff. But feeling the way I did about him there in the Grenadines, I seriously wondered if I would do the same thing again or if I would leave him for the sharks to sort out.

As everyone piled back into the sailboat, Bob didn't speak to me for the rest of the day. I was baffled and hurt by his behaviour. Our friends exchanged glances but said nothing.

+++

Around day five, we hit a storm, and Bob asked me to batten down the hatches of our stateroom, which I did. John went below and did the same with the rest of the portholes. We stayed topside to get through the worst of it and found our way into a protected inlet where we could moor for the night. Later, when we went down to our bedrooms, we were greeted with a flood. Water was sloshing back and forth across the floorboards, and everything was soaked, including the mattress in our stateroom. It's a wonder the boat didn't sink with all that water collected in the bilge. Apparently, there are two levels of battening down the hatches. One simply closes and locks the porthole, but there is also a deeper storm hatch that needs to be in place to keep the water out in rough seas. Who knew? I certainly didn't. Bob was furious with me.

We slept on a wet mattress that night, and Bob invoked one of his major pouting episodes. Of course, I felt terrible because I had messed up, but not on purpose; it was an honest mistake, but he couldn't see it that way. He'd been testy with me on the trip, but this was over the top. The next day, the tension in the sailboat was as thick as fog as he ignored me and barely spoke to anyone. John had been Bob's best friend since high school, so he knew his moods well. I remember John telling me what happened many years ago when Bob lost a Monopoly game they were playing. Bob was so pissed at him for taking his Boardwalk and Park Place that he stormed out of the house and didn't speak to John for a whole year. Ridiculous, but true.

I decided I'd had enough. Life was too short to put up with these increasingly unpredictable dark moods of his. In the past, I may have taken all the crap Rick threw my way, but not this time. I deserved to be treated better and would not be pulled back into who I used to be. I realized I had a choice, and this time around, I needed more in a relationship than what I was getting from Bob now. I still loved him, but I had loved Rick too, and love wasn't enough anymore.

The next day, we would be heading back across the Bequia Channel to St. Vincent, where we would catch our flight home. During that uncomfortable night of tossing and turning on a soggy mattress, I made up my mind. I was going to leave Bob. And as sad as that made me, I also felt a sense of relief. I was no longer that little girl who was afraid of standing up for herself. I deserved to be treated better, and I'd tell him when we got back home.

The next morning, we left our secluded lagoon and headed out. The storm was over, but gusty headwinds were still blowing hard, and the seas were rough. None of us were particularly nervous in the turbulence.

But there was something unsettling about how the waves became increasingly larger as we sailed deeper into the dark waters of the channel and the shorelines disappeared. Bob took the helm from the captain at one point, which made me nervous because he wasn't an experienced enough sailor, especially in these conditions. He began struggling to balance the boat when the wind suddenly ripped the mainsail off the mast. In seconds, it was torn to shreds. Without a mainsail, we were left with only a jib and a small motor to get us to St. Vincent.

The captain took over, and that's when things really got bad. We found ourselves in fifteen-to-twenty-foot waves, which I found utterly terrifying. With each swell, we would climb to the crest of the wave, which looked like a mountain of water, only to reach the top and plummet like a stone into the bottom of the trough on the other side. Growing up on Georgian Bay, I had no fear of choppy waters, but this was different. I was frightened for my life.

We were proceeding slowly, not only because of the swells but also because we were running without a mainsail. After about an hour of being tossed about like a matchstick in a tempest, I felt paralyzed with terror. The men seemed to be handling it well enough, but Lynda and I were not. We were too frightened to let go of the grab rails to get the life jackets stored under the seats. I slid down to the floor and wrapped my arms and legs around the steering column for stability. Sharp points of fear clawed at my chest, and I pulled my jacket up over my head so that I wouldn't have to look at the mountain of waves crashing around me. The captain reached down and patted me on the head. I asked how much more of this we needed to go through. His answer was not the one I wanted to hear.

"About another three hours, and we should be over the worst of it," he said. Three hours! I didn't think I could survive another three minutes.

I sat there on the wet deck thinking about my beloved daughter and contemplating my life and the possible end of it. I had such a feeling of desperation and vulnerability out in the middle of the sea. I was powerless in the unrelenting force of this massive ocean. I thought of the novena I'd made to save my daughter from leukemia and decided that was my best option for survival again. I'd broken with the Church after my experience with the nuns at Marymount, but my roots were still there, in that little Catholic church in Britt. Deep down, I still had enough faith to turn to God for help once again. I worried He might take exception to my appearance only for dire emergencies. But as the Danish philosopher Kierkegaard once said, "Faith sees best in the dark." So, right there in the middle of the raging Caribbean Sea, I asked God to get us home safely and in return, I promised to work hard at saving my marriage and find healthy ways to resolve conflict.

We did eventually arrive safely at the port in St. Vincent, and Lynda jumped out of the boat and kissed the dock. Bob put his arms around me and was talking to me again. I felt tired and raw, and he could see how wobbly and disoriented I was from the experience. We finally boarded our flight home. When we arrived in Toronto, I was relieved and thankful we'd gotten through it all. But I remained unnerved by the whole experience.

I said goodbye to the man I'd come close to having an affair with, telling him that I loved Bob and wanted to make my marriage work. He never spoke to me again. I wanted to remain friends, but his pissed-off silence spoke volumes, and I was relieved I'd aborted the relationship when I did. From that day on, I started feeling at peace with making things right. I focused on recalibrating my marriage and becoming softer toward Bob. I was determined to do this without losing myself in the process. I realized that despite his confidence and sizable presence, Bob had insecurities of his own. I needed to become better at giving him what he needed from me. And I needed to be more direct in telling him what I needed in return.

As I thought about it, I knew I was a big part of the problem with my laser focus on my job and obsession with getting ahead. I was often manacled to my work and vacant in body and mind. Bob simply pulled away and detached himself, rather than discussing it with me. I wanted to find constructive ways for us to open up and be honest with each other.

+++

When I was married to Rick, the way I dealt with him was through avoidance. I rarely confronted him or had any meaningful discussions about our relationship. I didn't ask questions, and deep down, maybe I didn't want to know the answers. I began to wonder if I was repeating the same pattern with Bob. I'd developed my own coping mechanisms, and more often than not, simply avoided engaging in his moods.

I realized I needed to change that to make our marriage work. Despite his behaviour on the sailing trip, I believed Bob was a keeper. He was a good person and a good dad to Andrea, which meant a lot to me because Rick was absent from her life so much.

So we talked. Bob wasn't a guy to express his feelings verbally, so he listened a lot more than he spoke. I told him I was confused by his behaviour, especially on the boat, and how I was hurt by his cold indifference. He told me one thing — he thought I was having an affair and would leave him like his first wife. And there it was in a nutshell. It wasn't a long talk, just an important one. I confessed I'd been tempted but put a stop to it before things progressed. He said that's all he could think about when he looked at me, which gave me a better understanding of why he acted the way he did.

Bob softened, but I knew his moods and stubbornness would always be a part of his DNA. So when they surfaced, I'd let him stew for a bit in his own juices. Then I'd put my arms around him and talk it out when he'd calmed down. He always responded in a loving manner, and I knew in my heart, he loved me. Sex had been a fiery part of our relationship since the day we met, and rekindling our intimacy was important to making things work too. I still found him sexy as ever. All we needed was a little "Ravel's Bolero" to get the juices flowing. I would sometimes write him little love notes or funny poems to make him laugh. I'd put them under his pillow or hide them inside a pocket or tucked into his briefcase. I began to realize that Bob's insecurities ran deep, and he needed constant confirmation of my love for him. I could do that.

It may have taken a storm on the high seas and a deal with the Almighty to save my marriage, but it also made me stop to think about what I was doing. What we were both doing. I realized that our relationship had shifted away from the passion and newness of the early days to the steady throb of everyday life. I saw how over time, love never stays the same; it changes and changes again. Not for the worse, just different. I believed we were worth saving and needed to remind myself that we had many more good times than bad. Bob and I both knew we had to work to make it work. I don't believe he ever cheated on me; I think we both put the brakes on at the same time.

My bargain with God was another good one, and not for a minute have I ever regretted it. I never told Bob about that promise and kept it with me all the years we were together. We had quietly drifted away from each other, and then thankfully, we drifted back.

CHAPTER 16

Critters, Snakes, and Secrets

I was sitting in an executive meeting on the fifty-sixth floor of Commerce Court looking out over the Toronto Harbour. It always amazed me that I'd made it into the high-powered world of banking and had my place with the group of movers and shakers sitting around the table. Sometimes, I felt like a fraud and wondered what I was doing there.

As the Head Office Vice President of Consumer Loans, I was one of twenty or so executives attending a meeting with the chairman of the bank and the president of the retail division. It was a command performance held each fiscal quarter to report the profits and losses of our divisions. I was one of two women present. My single female colleague suppressed a giggle when I whispered, "Do you think there are any long-term side effects from exposure to this much testosterone?" Men always had the dominant voice in any meeting like this. It was difficult to get airtime with so many navy blue suits and starched collars sitting around the table. The men used sports metaphors for everything and made references to golfing games they'd shared. There was a camaraderie that excluded the women in the room, and they made no attempt to bridge the gap. Women simply had to speak up and hold their ground. It was a skill that had to be honed and executed with dogged determination.

I looked at the masters of the universe sitting around the polished rosewood conference table and pictured them as badgers, foxes, weasels, and most definitely, a few wolves and vultures. I didn't mean it in a purely derogatory way; it was just something I did to amuse myself during those scripted meetings. Some of my male colleagues were quite nice, and I enjoyed a good working relationship with them. It helped to pass the time while I watched high-performance executives bend and stretch themselves into good corporate soldiers to say all the right things for the big guys.

With their various white-collar backgrounds and business degrees, what would they think of me if they knew of my humble beginnings or that I didn't even graduate from high school? Would my Métis roots make a difference in how they saw me? My sister Estelle told me people in her office called her "Little White Dove." She took it in her stride and smiled through it, as we were always taught to do.

Many of my colleagues had asked me where I went to university, and when I gave vague answers, I could see the judgment in their faces, and some looked embarrassed by my lack of an answer. I was proud that I had accomplished what I did without the formal education they had, but it still made me feel diminished by hiding the truth. One even asked me whom I'd slept with to get my position.

While I enjoyed the power trip of being there, sometimes I had the uneasy feeling that my work environment was slowly devouring my soul. I was getting older, and more and more, I was feeling the empty spaces I was creating between my daughter and me. I knew my job consumed me, but I was like a junkie, hooked on the high of knowing I was very good at what I did, and sometimes better than many of the men around me. So, despite the "devouring my soul" bit, I thrived on fitting in and being part of a group. My confidence continued to grow, and my developing leadership skills became my weapon of choice.

As a woman executive in an industry where men were traditionally king, I had clawed my way through many battles to get where I was. Sometimes, I turned down promotions when they offered me less in money and status than the man I was replacing. I'm sure they thought I was a real pain in the butt, and those refusals didn't win me any friends in the upper echelons, but I didn't care. In every case where I stood my ground, I was confident that I was the best candidate for the position. Eventually and reluctantly, they caved and gave me what I wanted. But it was usually a fight to get there. I kept a sticky note of my favourite quote on my desk that read *Illegitimi non carborundum.* (Don't let the bastards grind you down.)

I remember one incident where the head of one of the divisions asked me to replace my boss, who was moving on to another project. I said I would happily do that for the same pay grade and title as my boss. He told me that was impossible, that it would be a lateral move for me. He added that if I didn't accept his terms, it wouldn't look good and could affect my career. I stuck to my guns and said no thank you.

A week later, the same man gathered the staff on my floor together for an announcement. He told them I would be replacing my boss, effective immediately. I had no idea he was going to say that and had never accepted his terms. When I challenged him after the meeting, he simply said, "You got what you wanted. I hope you're happy," and walked away. And I was happy — I got the same pay grade and title as my predecessor.

Throughout my career, I met a lot of good people at CIBC, but I also experienced my share of gender inequality. In my earlier days, when I was a manager at head office, the company had a cafeteria in the building for all employees and another more sophisticated one for managers at a certain level. I was the only woman working in an open pod of men on a special project. For ease of communication, there were no walls around our desks. We all did the same work, but my grade level was one below the men. At noon, my colleagues would get up and go to the executive dining room, while I didn't qualify and had to go to the general employee cafeteria. I felt angry about it and tried without success to have the human resources department correct the disparity. When the men invited me to go with them as a guest, I refused and told them I would only go on my own merit.

I remember the day when one of the guys jokingly said, "C'mon, you can't expect to be the same grade as a man. Coming with us is the only way you'll ever be allowed in the dining room."

I responded by telling him, "We'll see about that. I'll get there. And one day you'll all be working for me." The executive dining room closed down before I made the grade. However, my prophecy came true, and over the next few years, most of those men did end up working for me.

⬥⬥⬥

People who worked in head office needed to communicate with the various regional executives across Canada, especially when a national program was being implemented. As a group, they resisted head office interference in anything regional and, understandably, felt they knew what was best for their provinces. I had a new consumer credit program I wanted to introduce across Canada. My team was a wonderful group of innovative thinkers, and they were proud of the project they had worked so hard to develop. It was something that would be good for the customer and profitable for the bank. Knowing the regional vice presidents could be resistant to national product changes, I travelled across Canada to every province and met with each executive in person. It went well, and I got full agreement from everyone, so I returned home ready to finalize the project.

Shortly afterwards, the same regional people were in Toronto for a meeting. I offered to attend and give them an update on the implementation timelines for the program. It should have been a slam dunk since they'd already agreed to the details of the proposal. But I'd heard they were always at their worst when they were in a pack. A colleague of mine warned me they were like a pit of vipers when they were all together in a room. I assured him I'd be fine because my attendance was just a courtesy to update them on the implementation of a project they'd already approved.

They crucified me.

They were collectively hostile and brought up nothing but roadblocks and complaints. They raised all the same issues we'd successfully resolved during my visit. But together in a room, I was their prey, and they were vicious. I'd left my husband and daughter and spent a week of my life travelling across Canada to get their buy-in, only to have them renege on our agreement and humiliate me. Back in my car, I broke down and blubbered my way back to the office. When I faced my staff and told them the project was cancelled, it felt like the day Rick left me alone to tell our employees we couldn't pay them.

I didn't often show weakness when it came to workplace challenges, but that experience broke me. I felt so deceived. I would remember that day as one of the worst moments of my career. My parents had always taught me the meaning of kinship and caring for our own. Was I not one of them? Had CIBC not become my family? I'd certainly given enough of my life to belong there. There were always a lot of difficult situations to manage at work, but for reasons I don't understand, I found that betrayal particularly brutal. Perhaps my reaction was magnified by my long hours and exhaustion. Or perhaps I wondered who I would need to become to accept this kind of duplicity from my colleagues. Without their work faces on, I'm sure these executives were all lovely enough people with their family and friends. But in a gang, they competed brutally to demonstrate their power, trying to outdo each other. I decided I didn't want that for me.

Thankfully, that incident happened the day before my vacation, and I couldn't get away fast enough. Bob and I left the next day for Gaston's White River Resort on the White River in Arkansas. It was one of our favourite places to go. He enjoyed fly fishing in the shallow streams while I sat under a tree to read, write, and watch a large colony of great blue herons nested in the trees.

⬩⬩⬩

During my twenty-five years in banking, I had a few good bosses and some despicable ones. I learned a lot from all of them. I even punched one of my male bosses in the stomach once when I thought he'd said something misogynistic to me. He was just an annoying kind of man and had been trying my patience for days. He was always in my office mansplaining things he thought I didn't understand. He was an MBA graduate and knew I didn't have his credentials. The constant smirk on his face irritated me. So that day, when he mumbled some innocuous thing, it bugged me, and I punched him. My violent reaction came out of nowhere. Honestly, it was like being back at the St. Lawrence Market swinging my bag of beans.

It turned out I misunderstood what he actually said, and thankfully he was gracious enough to forgive me when I apologized. He could have had me fired. From that point, I worked harder at tolerating him and became more vocal when he did things I found annoying. That seemed to work for both of us, and we began to get along better. The morning after it happened, I found a Louisville Slugger baseball bat on my desk, compliments of my colleague in human resources.

⬩⬩⬩

Aging in the workplace was a fully acceptable thing for men. But for women, our future prospects dimmed with each passing year. There was no tolerance for spider veins in the boardroom. I remember meeting a high-ranking female executive in the parking lot after she'd had a facelift. When I asked how she was doing, she said, "It was bloody hell! It's so unfair. They just don't let you get old in this game."

I had one female boss who had a serious drinking problem and terrified the staff with her cruelty and mood swings. I'd always held her in such high regard until I worked for her and saw her in action. It was a closely held secret inside her department, although even her own bosses witnessed many of her alcoholic embarrassments at staff Christmas parties. After my years with Rick, I'd had my fill of drunken rages. I spent a couple of years working for her, learning how NOT to be a boss, and then transferred to another area of the bank. That was the great thing about working for such a large company. You could move around and start over many times during your career. Perhaps because women had to work so hard to reach the senior ranks, we were often in fierce competition with one another. I found some of my female bosses to be the worst mentors. I guess they'd fought hard to get where they were and had no intention of making it easier on other women coming up the ladder.

I'll be forever grateful to one male boss who was a champion for me at CIBC as Miss Pitts was in my grade school days. He took every opportunity to help my career along. I followed him many times into new exciting projects, and we always worked well together. He was a big thinker, a visionary of new ideas and innovations, which was not my strong suit. But he was never a detail man, and that's where I fit in. I loved to get down in the weeds and work out the implementation of a project. We teamed up often and complemented each other's skill sets. He gave me full rein to work projects through and the freedom to succeed or fail. He taught me to trust both myself and the creative process. I was treated fairly, and he always had my back.

Despite the shortcomings of my own female bosses, I worked hard to support the women on my teams. I was proud of my record of support and respect for my employees at every level, including the janitorial staff. I never forgot that first day at Marymount College when Sister Mary Stella asked us to tell the class what our fathers did for a living. I went out of my way to chat with the night cleaners when I was working late. And I often found little homemade gifts from them on my desk.

Although it could be a tough place to survive and the stress overwhelming at times, there were many more good moments than bad. Overall, I loved my work, and I met many intelligent and creative people along the way, who made coming to work a joy. I was confident in my ability to work with talented teams to implement new and innovative ideas. Admittedly, the hours were long, and I had too often sacrificed my family and my health to get where I was. But that wasn't foremost on my mind at the time. I enjoyed the high I felt from seeing a difficult project through to implementation. And I loved the feeling of power that came with the title on my business card.

+++

My appointment to vice president happened about the same time I began experiencing severe joint pain, especially in my hands. The ache would start late in the afternoon and by evening, my fingers were so swollen and painful they looked like useless claws hanging at the end of my arms. I went from doctor to doctor, and no one could find anything wrong with me.

Some of them said it was stress-related and told me to quit my job and change my lifestyle. Just like that, as though they were telling me to switch breakfast cereals. My distrust of the medical profession still ran deep, and I didn't believe or listen to any of them. As the pain got worse, I saw myriad doctors: GPs, neurologists, hematologists, rheumatologists, and even a psychiatrist. They all found nothing, but I wouldn't give up. I knew something was wrong, and it wasn't in my head.

My health issues remained unresolved while the joint pain was getting worse. But I ignored it and chalked it up to arthritis. And while I was getting an increasing number of nosebleeds, I wasn't about to stop my life for something doctors couldn't find. Some days, I needed a cane to walk and would simply tell my colleagues I'd hurt myself playing racquetball. I didn't want anyone to know. Then one day, after a series of new tests, my rheumatologist at Mount Sinai finally confirmed a diagnosis. I had systemic lupus erythematosus, an autoimmune disorder where your body attacks its own tissues and organs. There was no cure, he said, and gave me pamphlets to read about this chronic disease.

Bob was devastated at the news. It frightened us both. He took me in his arms, and we lay down on the bed and slept without dinner. I didn't know what the future held for me, but there was one thing I knew for sure. My husband would be with me for the good times and the bad.

Lupus is called the disease of a thousand faces, and some research suggests it's more common in Indigenous women than Caucasian. The pain moved around my body and presented no specific pattern. It's no wonder doctors would often label lupus sufferers like me as hypochondriacs when both patient and doctors often couldn't pinpoint the pain. Little was known about the disease at that time, and few books had been written on the subject. But the more I educated myself with the limited information I could find, the more frightened I became. This was a very serious disease that could attack my kidneys, brain, lungs, and other organs as well as my joints. I needed to stay out of the sun, probably for the rest of my life. The UV rays could trigger a flare-up and even create nasty lesions on my skin. I'd been a sun worshipper my whole life, and I found this particularly hard to accept. My doctor said I had a milder form of lupus, and while there was no cure, he offered to put me on prednisone for preventative treatment. I was reluctant to start taking such a powerful steroid, so I refused and told him I would try to manage without it and see how the disease progressed.

✦✦✦

I continued to keep up with my work schedule and tried not to think too much about my condition. I took pain meds and worked through the effects of the disease, which had its ups and downs, but nothing as debilitating as what I'd read in the books. I managed to live my life in a pretty normal way, although staying out of the sun put a lot of limitations on our lives. I was thankful Bob loved being in the shade with me more than being in the sun without me. Outside of my family, I hid my illness well. In the often cutthroat world of banking, where only the mighty survive, there was no tolerance for weakness. I was convinced that if my fellow bankers sniffed out my illness, the corporate pack would abandon me like roadkill on the highway to executive nirvana.

We had a quiet room on our floor equipped with a single bed where employees could lie down to rest if they weren't feeling well. I would sometimes secretly go in there during the day and lock the door when the pain got bad. My secretary was the only one who knew where I was. And on the days I needed a cane to walk, I continued to tell people at work I'd hurt myself in one way or another. Sometimes, I had to wear a Holter monitor to check my heart rhythms. I remember once I had one on before attending a meeting of senior people. I ducked into the bathroom beforehand, scrambling to remove the device and stuff it into my briefcase before going into the conference room. I didn't want any questions.

I was finding that lupus was a strange disease where I could look perfectly normal on the outside while the illness raged on the inside.

After living with an alcoholic for so many years, I was well practised in the art of hiding the truth. To make matters worse, during that time, I was also going through menopause. I was often short-tempered, soaked with sweat from hot flashes, and suffering bouts of brain fog as thick as mud. Andrea and Bob kept their distance from me when I was at my worst to avoid being the target of my madness. My temper could flare at the slightest thing.

In 1995, I moved out of Consumer Loans and became Vice President of Electronic Banking. CIBC and the Loblaw grocery chain entered into a partnership to develop an innovative way of banking. We were going to build a virtual bank called President's Choice Financial. My team and I were part of this exciting venture. It would be a new way of banking and a new way of thinking. I was all in.

It was my dream job. I travelled with members of my team to England, Portugal, Spain, and various parts of the United States looking at software. I enjoyed my work more than ever and managed to keep my pain levels under control. Staying out of the sun could be tricky at times when I was travelling, but I managed it. I was in my glory, working with a team of bright individuals and learning new and exciting ways of doing business every day. Then eighteen months into the project, something happened that changed everything.

CHAPTER 17

From Pinstripes to Poetry

I was walking through the Atrium on Bay in downtown Toronto on my way back to my office upstairs. A picture in the window of an art shop caught my eye. The scene was of a beautiful pale yellow house set in a garden of pastel flowers and sloping hillsides. A rainbow of colours was reflected in the windows of the house in the painting. It was similar to the dreamlike images painted by Thomas Kinkade and not the usual type of art I liked.

As I looked at the picture, I ached to feel the stillness and beauty of that scene. I wanted to smell the clover in the fields and listen to the birds. That house was where I wanted to be. I could see myself spending time with my family in a peaceful place like that. I wanted to be surrounded by those beautiful gardens. The picture's peaceful scene stirred the comforting warmth I felt when I thought about my little house in Britt so long ago. I went into the shop, purchased the picture, and loaded it in my car before going back to work. That's when I started to think about retirement. As with Mr. Powell, this was a crossroads, and I knew in that moment, I had a choice about how I wanted to live the rest of my life, a choice that was both exciting and scary.

I was only fifty-two. All reason told me I was too young to retire and anyway, what would I do if I did leave the bank? I'd been working since I was sixteen. I didn't know anything else but work. Several years before, the bank had sent me to the Ivey Business School at Western University for a three-week intensive executive program, like a mini MBA. I found it exhausting to be in class Monday to Saturday from 8:00 a.m. to 10:00 p.m., and then retire to my room and work halfway through the night on homework assignments. But I loved every minute of it.

I'd worked so hard to get where I was. How could I give up my six-figure salary, annual stock options, and the executive perks and bonuses? My identity had become the title on my business card, and

I enjoyed the respect that came with it. In my social life, when people asked what I did, I felt instant admiration. Even the car I drove belonged to CIBC. They paid for all my gas and car expenses. Could I really walk away from all that? I thought it was time to discuss it with Bob.

I knew he would have trouble understanding why I'd ever consider retiring. Two years before, when Bob turned sixty, the Royal Bank did some downsizing, and he was forced into early retirement. As part of the management team, he was offered a good package, but the news crushed him. This sudden change of direction made him feel smaller, less of the person he was. He was not ready to retire and fell into a dark depression, feeling worthless and abandoned. I helped drag him out of it as much as I could, but he looked like a lost soul when I headed out to work each day.

When boredom just became too much, Bob offered to help a few friends with renovation projects and discovered he was really good at it. He'd had some practice renovating his own house but hadn't done much else. He started taking on jobs commercially and became busy and energetic, leaving the house every day carrying his toolbox instead of a briefcase. As much as he was still bitter about being forced to retire, I could tell he was happier than he'd been in a long time, doing something he enjoyed.

Bob had quit smoking decades before, but during his "construction phase," he took to having the odd cigar when he was hanging with the boys or at home on the deck. Bob's personality changed with a stogie perched in the side of his mouth. He would lean back in his chair looking pensive and superior with his chin held high, like a mob boss surveying his domain. He developed a seriously know-it-all attitude when he smoked, like a blending of Al Capone and Winston Churchill. Andrea and I would tease and mock him mercilessly, but it didn't faze him. It was so foreign to who he was, and that made it all the funnier. Occasional cigars or not, Bob had found a different world, and he smiled a lot more living his new life.

Could there be a new life somewhere out there for me? What would I do and who would I be without my title, my network, and my CIBC social grid? I certainly didn't want to be Bob's drywall assistant. How could I survive arriving naked at mid-life without a strategic plan on how to reinvent myself? I'd had a lot to prove during my climb to vice president, both to my colleagues and to myself. That little Métis girl was kicked to the curb a long time ago to make room for the tougher corporate soldier I'd become. But how did that corporate soldier perform as a mother?

+++

Andrea was an independent latchkey kid, never expecting me to be home every night for dinner. In spite of this, she had grown into a beautiful young woman, now working at a publicity firm in Toronto. I would get a raw feeling in the pit of my stomach when I thought about how much time I'd lost with her and would never get back. This had been on my mind a lot, and as hard as I had ignored the feelings in the past, more and more, my heart overflowed with guilt. I'd given my daughter a good life of comfort, and as an only child, she wanted for nothing. But she was alone a lot when we moved around during my marriage to Rick and then again during all the times I left her when I was away on business trips or travelling with Bob. Andrea would often eat alone or go to a friend's place for a sleepover when I worked late at the office. While I took on the task of pushing myself uphill on Bay Street to prove I belonged there, did my daughter feel ignored and did she resent my absences?

If she did, Andrea showed me nothing but love, kindness, and respect. Even as a teenager, I never experienced any of the screaming matches and moments of "I hate you" many of my colleagues were dealing with at home. Still, while I gave myself high marks for competency and bottom-line results at work, I couldn't do the same for my performance as a parent. As the mother of this beautiful girl, I regretted all my missed opportunities.

I found it a difficult subject to think about, so I expressed myself through poetry. I remember the Saturday morning when I wrote this poem. Andrea was lying on the sofa beside me. She was twenty-four by this time and had come home to recharge her batteries.

Rewind

Freeze frame, a picture.
Outside the window, snow falls.
Hypnotic puffs cling together,
Dancing slowly to the ground.
Inside, a fire dances.
A room warm as bath water.
I sit reading.
Curled up in the corner of my couch.
Tights, sweatshirt, no bra,
Absorbed in the Financial Post.
I look up and feel a thunderbolt.
She sleeps, long legs stretched out,
Filling the space beside me.
I feel a love so fierce,
It bursts in my chest like an explosion.
The fire snaps,
The snow continues to fall.
My daughter, my friend,
My baby, my life.
Boomerang kids they call them.
They leave to find their way,
They get lost and come back home.
They stay until the emptiness is gone.
I watch her sleep.
I want her to be six months,
Six years, sixteen years,
Anything but twenty-four.
A haunting verse from a lullaby I wrote
When she was 3 months old:
"My child, my love, my baby,
My precious little song,
Come let me hold and love you,
Before you're grown and gone."
I need to go back.
I can't count them all.
The days I took for granted,
The days I thought would last forever.
The conferences, the working weekends,
The cold dinners, the babysitters…
If I could rewind,
If I could play it back
The way it should have been,
This ache in my chest might stop hurting.

In the coming days, I thought a lot about the often vicious politics of my work and my secret battle with lupus to keep in step with the pack. Although my illness was pretty much under control, my doctor warned me that stress could be a trigger for flare-ups. I worried the demands and raw edges of my job would make the disease worse, and I'd be forced to retire the hard way. Thoughts about retirement invaded my consciousness like magpies, prattling on until I couldn't deny the reality of the message. I'd sit in my den at home and stare at that enchanting yellow house in the picture. Could I make that happen for me? Could there be life beyond the boardroom?

Sometimes, I'd wake in the middle of the night with heart palpitations and a need to recalculate my investment portfolio. I wondered if freedom really does come at fifty-five, as all the old television commercials promised. Freedom 55 ads ran for years, and everyone felt the impact of the clever marketing propaganda, as it bang-bang-banged away like a jackhammer at the psyches of good working people. I knew about marketing tactics. It's all about rewiring our brains so that our hearts and wallets will follow like lemmings to the investment pool. They said if everyone invested wisely and followed the rules of the game, people could retire to enjoy suntans, endless games of golf, and oceanfront hot tubs. It promised us freedom from life's miseries when we arrived at the magic age of fifty-five. It was all head games, and millions of people swallowed it hook, line, and Jacuzzi. So now, at the ripe old age of fifty-two and after many ups and downs in the market, my financial planner and my RRSP portfolio all confirmed I had not yet come of age. But how much is enough? Does it ever stop?

+++

Sometimes, it felt like I'd been running a marathon ever since I left the shores of Georgian Bay forty years ago. I worked hard to survive, to fit in, and to prove myself worthy of my accomplishments. I'd found a new identity in my job, one that brought me money, status, and recognition. I was tougher and more driven than my two sisters and my brother, and my life experiences were wildly different. Estelle and I were most similar in personality while Bruce and Maureen shared a more serious disposition. But the four of us remained as close as ever. We kept in regular contact, and every summer when I went back to Britt for my week with the girls, my heart would soften at the sight of the old Gereaux Lighthouse and the cobalt blue waters of the bay. Sometimes inspired by the natural beauty of my surroundings, I'd do some writing when I was there.

I had a growing number of stories and poems stuffed in a wooden box at the back of my closet. I'd kept everything, including some gut-wrenchingly sad things I wrote when I was married to Rick. There were several poems about my life as a little girl, sitting in a strawberry field, swimming off the dock at the boathouse, and tobogganing in the snow. I realized how privileged my life had become when I read those simple snapshots of a life I used to have so long ago. I longed to remember what it felt like to be that girl again. She seemed to visit me when I was writing; I could feel her presence in my words.

One Saturday morning, I was in my den drinking a cup of tea and staring at the picture of the yellow house. As I sat in my rocking chair, I let myself imagine what it would be like to live there and not have to go to work in the morning. I found it difficult to see myself as a lady who watches the traffic gridlock on morning television rather than being stuck in the middle of it. The deeper I thought about these things, the harder I rocked, just like when I was a child. Sitting in a rocking chair never lost its magic for me. The back and forth movement always helped me to relax and think. At the same time, writing made me feel alive and in touch with a side of myself that gave me joy. I began to realize how much I longed to have the time in my life to write out the stories and poems that were trapped in my imagination. While I rocked and projected myself into that picture on the wall, a little poem began to form in my head. I wrote it down, word for word, exactly as it poured out of my pen.

Alliance

An alliance with our inner voice is waiting,
To take its turn when dreams are lost to dust.
We look inside and find cobwebs of purpose,
Forgotten as the idols turn to rust.

A voice in time, a tiny speck of vision,
Breaks through the fog and touches deep within,
A magic long forgotten to a memory,
Of special times where promises begin.

We listen with a heart possessed and wonder,
The simple truth enlightened by the soul,
A precious chance to have our voice of wisdom,
Within our grasp to cherish and to hold.

The words in that poem, coming from somewhere inside, were telling me it was time to slow down and change the pace of my life. My illness was a major factor, but so was my desire to be more present for my husband and daughter. I wanted more for myself too: time to explore the parallel universe around me, to find life beyond the boardroom. It was at that moment right there in my rocking chair that I knew what I had to do. I had climbed the mountain, and now it was time to plant the flag and enjoy the view.

✦✦✦

I finally talked to Bob about my taking early retirement, and as I expected, he didn't get it.

"Despite how much I love this renovation work, if the bank called me, I'd go back tomorrow," he said. His pride was still bruised, so I knew he would have a difficult time understanding. Bob was always proud of me for achieving the title of VP. But even when I made more money than he did, there was never any resentment. He enjoyed telling people what I did at CIBC and loved to celebrate my accomplishments.

We talked endlessly, and Bob tried hard to understand my decision. But after the pain and suffering he had gone through, he was concerned about how I would handle life without my job to go to. While he worried about my health, I sensed he also worried, as I did, about the loss of income. We'd become used to the financial perks that came with my title. Bob tried hard not to push on that point and left the decision up to me. He said he'd support whatever I wanted to do.

After months of vacillation, I made my decision. It was time to cut the corporate umbilical cord and announce my retirement. I took my boss for lunch, and while he ate his smoked meat sandwich, I told him about my plans. We'd enjoyed a good working relationship for many years, and he was surprised by the news. Knowing me and how dedicated I was to the job, I could tell he didn't believe I'd really go through with it. I gave him one year's notice and promised I would take our CIBC/Loblaw partnership project, President's Choice Financial, to the pilot stage before I left. I kept my retirement decision a secret from the rest of my colleagues and planned to make the official announcement closer to the date.

+++

In my final year at CIBC, I slowed down my pace at work and made time in my schedule to prepare for a new life. I attended writing classes at Ryerson (now Toronto Metropolitan University) on weekends and in the evenings. I hired a private writing coach and signed up for workshops and writing retreats. I joined the Storytellers School of Toronto and attended courses and group-sharing sessions on weekends. One of the boldest things I did was to take a leap of faith and attend a five-week Second City Improv workshop. This was way out of my comfort zone, but after so many years in the banking world, I desperately needed to loosen the tension in my body and the corporate grip on my left brain.

I was the oldest person in a room full of young aspiring actors. It was a gutsy move, and despite my age, I dug in. The first time the instructor put me in a group in front of the class with a random scenario and told us to improvise, I thought I would faint. But the laughter from the onlookers calmed me down, and it didn't take me long to realize how easily I could step into a role if I let myself go. I wasn't anywhere near as good as my younger classmates, but I had a ball. I was so impressed with the course that I hired the Second City Improv group to run workshops for my team at CIBC. It was a great way to release creativity in an environment where new thinking was critical to our success.

+++

When the time came to announce my decision at work, I was met with a healthy mix of shock and envy. Some queried me with cautious looks and a desperate need to rationalize my decision. They asked if I'd been downsized or right-sized, or if I was just downright mad. They were all still building their nest eggs for that well-planned retirement and couldn't imagine abandoning the golden handcuffs we all wore. Then there were all the questions. "Will you go to Florida?" "Are you going to consult?" "Won't you be bored?" "What will you do all day?"

"I'm going to write poetry," I answered. I loved to watch them squirm with discomfort at my jarring change of direction. My mind was made up. It was time to switch gears and listen to my body from the inside out.

✦✦✦

While retirement may have been the term used by the old corporate dogs that ruled the ranks for generations, I was determined to find life beyond the boardroom. How many times had I heard about men who retired and then disappeared into that great cotton-head abyss of white shoes and polyester pants? Perhaps it was time to change the perspective on this important life decision. Armed with a sense of pioneering spirit, I decided a different word was needed to describe the new life ahead of me.

At my retirement party, I stood up to the large group of two hundred staff and colleagues assembled for the event and announced that I wasn't retiring at all. After the gasps died down, I told them the word retire meant "hibernate," "go into seclusion," "be put out to pasture" or "go out of circulation." I continued by telling them I would rather do the opposite of all that. Instead of saying I'm retiring, I told them, I'd like to think of myself as arriving at an important destination. Then to a room full of hoots and hollers, I said, "I look forward to jumping headlong into my arrivement instead."

I said my goodbyes, and the gifts and flowers were loaded into my car. I headed for home, feeling as naked as a pinstripe suit without a business card. It was time to make plans for my arrivement and this remarkable gift of new beginnings.

Part Four (1998–2010)

No matter how talented a woman may be, or how useful in the church or society, if she is an indifferent housekeeper it is fatal to her influence, a foil to her brilliance and a blemish in her garments.

— *The Home Cook Book*, Toronto: Rose-Belford Publishing Company, 1881

CHAPTER 18

Domestic Bliss

In 1998, during the first year of my arrivement, I wanted to experience the many things I'd missed out on for so many years, especially the joys of learning how to cook. But my uncharacteristic burst of domesticity seemed to unnerve my family.

"Give her a wide berth," Bob told Andrea as I jumped from the kitchen stool to check on the contents of my new slow cooker.

"She bought a crockpot?" Andrea asked, lurching backwards to get out of my way.

Bob continued as though I wasn't in the room. "And that's not all. She has two boxes of Mason jars in the basement. She wants to 'do down' dill pickles and green tomato relish like her Aunt Muriel used to make."

Andrea stared at him. "Do you remember the last time she made dill pickles? She actually peeled the cucumbers before putting them in the jars. She told us the white cucumbers would turn green and that's when we'd know they were ready to eat. Of course they never did, and the whole batch went into the garbage."

"Geez, she's even wearing an apron" was all Bob could say, as their eyes remained locked on my every move. I even caught them rolling their eyes, but I couldn't blame them for worrying about my strange behaviour. Poor things, it was all so sudden. After so many years of working, I was determined to experience the full impact of domestic bliss.

So there I was, ready to do the wife and mother thing, and all they could do was stare at me all goggle-eyed amid the rich scent of my boneless rump roast. The kitchen had never been my best room. I'd always preferred the word processor to the food processor. Several years ago, when we were both still working, Bob threatened to turn the kitchen into a library if I didn't start cooking more often. I told him I thought that was a fine idea. So out of self-preservation, he donned an apron and learned to cook. He turned out to be good at it and found that he enjoyed preparing the meals. The kitchen had been saved, and I was a happy woman. But now, even though I'd always preferred the smell of a good book to the scent of braised pork ribs, I was ready to learn the art of running a household.

My family trod softly, perhaps suspecting that my cooking obsession might just be more menopause madness. I ignored them and continued on my journey. I washed the laundry in logical colour combinations, organized the kitchen shelves, cleaned out closets, and dusted every piece of bric-a-brac I could find — all this while stuffed red peppers cooked silently in my new state-of-the-art crockpot. I approached my household responsibilities with the same appetite as I had my banking career. I savoured the goodness of field-ripened tomatoes and the emotional harmony that flowed from a clean, organized home. The routine seemed to take on a rhythm of its own. Unfortunately, while I harvested these revelations along with my bounty of summer vegetables, my family remained perplexed by my newfound passions.

+++

We all remembered one of my earlier attempts at cooking that had not gone well. It happened two weeks before Christmas on a Saturday morning in 1991. I was flopped down on the sofa by the fire with the holiday edition of *Canadian Living* magazine. As I turned the pages, drinking in the glossy treats and treasures, I was suddenly thrown back into nostalgia about my mother's Christmas traditions. There on page forty-nine was an oven-perfect photograph of, complete with a recipe for, a tempting French-Canadian tourtière. It even had pictures of step-by-step cooking instructions.

The caption in the magazine read "What could be more scrumptious than a heart-warming, home-cooked meat pie on a cold snowy Christmas Eve?" I thought about my childhood and how the Christmas holidays had always been such a special time in my family. I thought about my mom and how she would set aside a special weekend every December for cooking a big batch of Christmas tourtière. That meat-pie-making ceremony was always an exciting time since it marked the beginning of our Christmas season.

I could still smell the tantalizing mixture of herbs, spices, and sizzling pork that filled the house and launched us into the festive spirit. I could feel the warmth of my family sitting around the small kitchen, cutting, slicing, and hatching holiday plans. I could hear my brother and father planning their yearly excursion into the woods for the best tree ever, see how they tied the leather straps of Dad's old wooden snowshoes to their boots, and hear as they crunched their way through the deep snow. I will never forget the holiday scent of a fresh balsam fir standing in a pail of water tied to the living room wall with string.

Seeing that tourtière recipe reminded me of what Christmas meant in those days. It was about food mostly and the ritual meals Mom made to celebrate the spirit of the season with family and friends. It was about finding oranges and hard candy in my stocking on Christmas morning and eating sticky homemade fudge with my brother and sisters. And it was always about Mom's luscious tourtière in the warming oven that welcomed everyone home from church on Christmas Eve.

So, when I looked at that tempting meat-pie recipe in the magazine, I was a little worried, knowing full well that my culinary skills did not extend to making tourtière.

However, after reading the "simple-to-follow-step-by-step" cooking lesson, I was determined to catch the flailing baton of my French heritage. I would teach my teenage daughter how to cook this wonderful meat pie and carry on the family tradition I'd enjoyed so much as a child.

How hard could it be?

I bought all the ingredients, and the next day, armed with the magazine recipe for making tourtière, my daughter and I ventured forth into the kitchen.

"Do you know what you're doing?" Andrea asked me, looking over my shoulder at the recipe. "You've never cooked one of those before, have you?"

"No, but we'll figure it out together," I told her, intent on doing my mother proud.

Perhaps I aimed too high. The first mistake I made was to multiply the recipe to make ten pies! I remembered how my mother always made several pies simultaneously, so I was following in my mom's kitchen slippers. What a muddled mess!

As my daughter and I furiously chopped, browned, and sliced, pans began to overflow. Twenty pounds of sizzling ground pork was spitting and exploding on the stove, like a hundred angry firecrackers.

The grease splattered on the wall and chunks of meat were bouncing out of the pan onto the floor.

"There's no more room in the skillet!" I said, pulling more cooking pans from the cupboard. "Quick! Start scooping some of the pork into another pot. Just leave the mess to clean up later."

Andrea slipped in the grease on the floor. "Oh my God, Mom!" Then she put her hand on my shoulder. "Maybe we should wait for Bob," she said.

"We can do this," I told her, as I spooned the meat into ever-larger pots and skillets. "I just miscalculated a bit!"

Andrea looked around the kitchen and grinned. "You think?"

"We can't stop now. We're just getting started. We'll get the hang of it. Let's get chopping and peeling! We need thirty onions," I told her.

"Thirty onions? I hate onions!" She squirmed in protest. "Peeling onions really hurts my eyes!"

I looked at my daughter and grinned. "Not the way we're going to peel them," I told her, running down the basement stairs. I was back in a jiffy with snorkelling gear. A few minutes later, Bob walked into the kitchen and stopped dead in his Wallabees. His eyes darted around the kitchen, now a tourtière-induced war zone.

"This looks more like 'torture' than 'tourtière,' girls," he said. "Why are you both wearing snorkel masks?"

Andrea grinned at Bob through her steamed-up goggles and pointed her knife in my direction.

"The masks were my idea," I called out to him while I vigorously peeled and chopped onions into a pile on the counter.

"No doubt," he answered.

"I don't know how to use your fancy chopper-thingy to dice these onions, so we're doing it the old-fashioned way with a knife. The masks really help to keep our eyes from watering. Brilliant, don't you think?"

"That chopper-thingy is a food processor," Bob said, not taking his eyes off me. "And I'm very glad you didn't try to use it," he added, drawing out his words like he was talking to a toddler. Bob looked at his daughter, who looked back at him from inside her mask.

"The mask really works," she told him. "It's a great idea."

He put his arm around me. "I could get a court order to stop you from teaching her how to cook," he whispered in my ear. Then he kissed Andrea on her snorkel mask and put the fire extinguisher on the counter before he left the kitchen.

"Can you even see out of that thing?" I asked her, peeking into my daughter's steamed-up snorkel mask. We were nose to nose, our lips stretched into a grimace by the suction of the masks. We stared at each other like fish in an aquarium. Then, building slowly but steadily, our giggles rose to a crescendo of hoots and screeches, as we pointed at each other. Bent over in belly pain, we looked around at the meat-pie hell we'd created. We held each other and shook with laughter and collapsed into a heap on the floor.

Eventually, all ten meat pies did get made on that Sunday afternoon, although the cleanup took some time. Surprisingly, the pies were edible, but our tourtière skills would improve over time. That meat-pie-making ritual went on to become a holiday tradition in our family for decades to come. Today, we still make multiple pies at one time, but with a large pot to accommodate the meat-overflow problem. The routine is like a tourtière-inspired assembly line. Each person participating in the cooking event has a specific job to do, browning the meat, chopping the vegetables, or preparing the spices. And despite the new invention of cooking goggles, we still wear snorkel masks to chop the onions.

✦✦✦

Hence, it was understandable that my husband and daughter were worried about my sudden attack of domesticity. But so far, I was proud of my accomplishments as a homemaker and happy with how far I'd come since I'd retired the year before. I'd learned a lot about the art of housekeeping, the value of having family meals together, and being home for my husband and more available for Andrea. Although she was working and living in her own apartment, she came home often. Daughters need their mothers at any age.

My career as a Martha Stewart-wannabe was a delicious indulgence, but not the occupation I wanted to take on for the rest of my life. It was a welcome respite from the hard-knock world of testosterone and bottom lines I'd left behind. It opened my eyes to a parallel universe, where I could find joy in the smallest of tasks and fulfilment in cooking for my loved ones. In the days ahead, I would continue to value the importance of family dinners, but Bob did most of the cooking. I happily took off my apron and got ready to find a new adventure.

CHAPTER 19

Changes and Big Announcements

We found a charming French country home in Cobourg, Ontario, on two acres of land, with a creek running through the back of the property. The house was about four times the size of our place in the Beach. It was surrounded by beautiful flower gardens and the exterior of the home was pale yellow, much like the picture I'd purchased that urged me to retire. I didn't connect the dots about the picture and my attraction to this house until we settled in. But I guess my subconscious had been hard at work.

If someone had told me a few years earlier that I would leave Toronto to move to the country, I would have dismissed the idea as lunacy. Small-town living was never for me, and Bob loved everything about a big city. But there we were making plans to do something neither of us had ever imagined we would do. Cobourg wasn't as small as some towns; it had a population of eighteen thousand people, and Port Hope was ten minutes away with another fifteen thousand. Cobourg was only an hour and a half away from downtown Toronto, so we still felt connected to the city. Like two excited children, we moved into our new home at the end of July 2000. On closing day, we walked down to admire our gurgling creek, holding a glass of champagne, like gentry to the manor born.

It was an exciting summer. Andrea was married on September 2, one month after we moved to Cobourg. I loved Sean, her new husband, and couldn't have asked for a better son-in-law. Andrea was a beautiful bride, and the wedding was an elegant affair at a small boutique hotel in Port Credit. Bob and I were happy to see her so much in love. Life was moving along, as it should.

+++

There were a lot of gardens to tend at our new home. I spent many hours with my hands in the dirt and got lost in the joy of it. Because of my lupus condition, I still had to be very careful in the sun, so I followed the shade around the house to do my gardening work. I'd been retired for two years by then, and my joint pain was significantly reduced. I'd also found an excellent homeopath right after I retired, and her remedies were producing very positive results. I had no need to take prescription drugs to control the pain.

With my new life well underway, I spent more time writing in my lovely office on the main floor overlooking the gardens. I'd already written several editorials for the *Toronto Star* since I retired and a few articles for various magazines. So, I decided to write my first children's picture book, *The Whoosh of Gadoosh*. It was about a woman who was homeless, who pushed her cart filled with magic buttons along the city streets. The children would go "whooshing" with her when they sneezed. They called her "Gadoosh," the same nickname kids gave an eccentric old woman in Britt when I was growing up. I was inspired to write the story after being moved by a woman I saw on my way to work every morning. She just stood on the sidewalk with her cart, smiling and waving at the cars. I wondered about her — who she was and how that ritual had become her life. I had a lot of misgivings about writing the story echoing in my brain, because I worried the subject of a woman experiencing homelessness would not be kid-friendly. But I ignored my inner critic, finished the manuscript, and sent it to a variety of publishers. Illumination Arts Publishing in Bellevue, Washington, picked up my book.

The Whoosh of Gadoosh was published as a large picture book with a beautiful jacket and colourful illustrations. The back cover had endorsements by Deepak Chopra, Dr. Bernie Siegel, Dr. Jampolsky, and Patty Hansen. Gadoosh made her debut in May 2002 at the BookExpo trade show at the Jacob Javits Convention Center in New York City. I'll never forget the thrill I got when I signed my books for long lines of people. I didn't know it at the time, but Bob was like a barker at a circus, herding crowds toward my booth from down the hall. He was the best!

The Whoosh of Gadoosh went on to win the Benjamin Franklin Award in the United States for the "Best New Voice" category. Zoe Mae Productions of Montreal also optioned the book for a TV cartoon series and pitched it to Corus Entertainment, who showed a lot of interest. I wrote a few sample scripts for Zoe Mae, Nelvana developed a storyboard for the Treehouse TV audience, and we were ready to sign the contract. Then at the last minute, Corus pulled the plug and decided to go with something more mainstream. My Gadoosh character was a bit of an oddball. Perhaps I was channelling my oddball Grandma Charron. In spite of my disappointment, it was a thrilling experience.

✦✦✦

In the same year my book was born, I had an even bigger birth to celebrate. My granddaughter, Farrell Shannon, came into our lives on August 2, 2002. Bob and I were overwhelmed with love for this beautiful child. Andrea, Sean, and Farrell lived two hours away in Oakville, and Bob and I spent a lot of time over the next couple of years travelling the highway. They would often come to Cobourg and stay, sometimes leaving Farrell with us for a week or so. My love for my granddaughter inspired me to write an article called "Farrell's Fire," which was published in several newspapers. It was about how I would teach her to live a life of inspiration. She was fifteen months old at the time.

✦✦✦

Becoming a grandmother to Farrell gave me a second chance. I'd missed so much with Andrea, and while I could never give my daughter those days back, perhaps being there for my daughter's daughter might allow me to fill some of those gaps. Farrell was a blessing of epic proportions for both Bob and me. We couldn't get enough of that kid. I taught her to dance in the rain in her pyjamas, gave her popsicles to eat in the bathtub, and made up songs with her on the lawn swing. We built villages from cardboard I saved in the garage, and we lay in bed and made up stories to tell each other. To the dismay of her parents, I taught her never to wear matching socks, as a sign of her individuality and creativity.

She was full of energy, and she made up special games to play with Bob. Even when he wasn't well, she would sit on the pillow next to him on the bed and talk to him. Once when she was four years old, I walked into the bedroom during one of these sessions.

Farrell said, "Excuse me, Nanny, but could we have some privacy? I'm telling Poppy all my favourite bad words." Poppy was beaming with joy.

✦✦✦

Our life in Cobourg was happy, quiet, and peaceful. We made some good friends and thoroughly enjoyed the slower lifestyle. I continued to write, and over the next few years, I published three more children's books with Orca Book Publishers.

Bob joined the local Probus Club, a social club for retired professionals. I kept busy serving on various boards: the Cobourg newspaper, the Cobourg Public Library, and the Northumberland Child Development Centre. I wrote for several newspapers and magazines, including a monthly editorial for the local paper and a regular column for children called Rhyme Stones for Kids. I started a writing group with five wonderful women from the area, and we met monthly to discuss our work and prop one another up. I felt like a different person, awakening to a new life in a reimagined world that I loved. I considered it a reward for the many years I'd spent living on the edge. But we were getting older, and after ten years, the house got too much for us to handle. It was time for another change.

Part Five (2010–2019)

We are resilient as a weed and beautiful as a wildflower.

— Christi Belcourt

CHAPTER 20

Making Adjustments

Looking back on the decade we spent in Cobourg, I realize how impactful my time there had been. Once the newness of retirement kicked in, I'd come to Cobourg still wondering if I needed to live in a big city with a big job and a big salary to be happy. But living in that small town gave me a bigger life than I could have ever imagined, and I discovered the joy of doing small things with great love. It gave me room to open myself up and look inside to find my magic while being the best I could be as a wife, a mother, a grandmother, a sister, a friend, and a writer.

⬩⬩⬩

We moved and settled into a condo in Oakville to be closer to our daughter and granddaughter. Bob and I quickly realized that downsizing to an adult lifestyle building was an enormous adjustment with many strict rules. In a community-based living arrangement, it's hard to get people to agree on anything. When Bob and I voiced an opinion or a suggestion, we were mostly ignored. I came to realize that old corporate dogs never die; they simply resurface on condo boards. We learned that we couldn't always get our own way, we couldn't renovate without condo board approval, and we had to live with dirty windows until the scheduled cleaning time. But we also learned that we could enjoy the snow without shovelling it, we could feel safe and secure, and we could swim in a warm pool in the middle of a snowstorm. Condo life offered us an opportunity to meet people with rich and interesting backgrounds in any number of social activities.

⬩⬩⬩

Living in a condo surrounded by older people was sometimes a painful reminder of where we were heading. We were aging like the rest of our generation, and it wasn't just my living space that had gotten smaller. I seemed to be shrinking more with each passing day. As I became a more compact version of myself, my doctor told me my spine was compressing, my dentist told me my gums were receding, and my stylist said my hair was thinning. And of course I was living closer to the ground without my height-boosting pumps.

Bob always loved my high-heeled shoes, especially one pair I bought in the eighties: a pair of burgundy-red patent leather stilettos with ankle straps and four-inch heels. When I'd cleaned out my closet over the years, he always insisted I keep those as a memento of my foxier days. He called them my "hooker boots." The shoes surfaced again when we moved into our condo. Sometimes, I'd put them on and sit beside him with my feet up in my recliner so that he could reminisce about the days of old. I wore them only in the chair; I couldn't even walk across the room in them anymore.

+++

We saw much more of Andrea and Sean, who lived only ten minutes away. We took Farrell to the local parks, and she stayed with us for regular sleepovers. Farrell and I went swimming several times a week in my condo swimming pool, and she made me laugh at her shenanigans in the water.

Since I began writing books for children, I'd been visiting elementary schools and doing readings in gymnasiums packed with hundreds of kids at a time. I had special shawls made to correspond with the theme of each story. The kids loved watching my wardrobe changes throughout my school presentations. After we moved to Oakville, when Farrell was in grade 3, I volunteered to do class readings of my books at her school. The following year, I held Author Teas, where I conducted lunchtime creative writing workshops for grades 4 to 6. Farrell was my helper, and we planned these events together. I continued working with Farrell's school for six years until she finished grade 8.

The rewards of having Andrea and her family close by quickly overturned any misgivings we had about the move. Slowly, we melded into the new lifestyle we'd chosen, and it wasn't long before we knew we'd done the right thing. It took us a full year to feel totally comfortable and settled, but we got there, and I was proud of us for taking this enormous step. Little did we know what a blessing our timing would be. Over the next ten years, we would hit a few bad patches and would need to be close to family and good medical facilities.

+++

From a health perspective, we got off to a rocky start in Oakville. Bob had a stroke about two years after we moved in. Thankfully, it was a minor one, but he lost his peripheral vision and his driver's licence, a devastating blow to his manhood. When I went into a store and left him in the car, he wanted to put a sign on the dashboard that read "My Wife Parked This Car." He was embarrassed to be associated with my unique parking skills. At the same time, I was experiencing bouts of severe chest pains and had half a dozen ambulance rides to the hospital, certain I was having a heart attack. Eventually, the doctors determined it was my gallbladder and not my heart, so that was an easy fix. But it wasn't so easy for Bob to fix his licence. It took him eighteen months of constant field vision tests to get it back and be able to drive again. He was like a man reborn when he finally got back behind the wheel.

+++

Rick was in and out of Andrea's life, having left Seattle to come back to Toronto. He and his fourth wife had split, and he was living alone in an assisted living apartment. Rick was in rough shape physically, but he could still be very charming and hadn't lost that wacky sense of humour Andrea always enjoyed. He never did fulfill his lifelong dream of making it big; he'd wasted his life and four marriages trying. He was still smoking despite having emphysema, and the drinking never really stopped. Andrea had come to terms with who he was years ago, and Bob had easily stepped into the dad shoes and worn them well. But she still felt a strong connection to Rick and did what she could to maintain contact with him. Between the two of them, Andrea was always the adult in the room. She knew how self-destructive he could be.

Rick was given an oxygen tank to use at home to help him to breathe on the condition he would stop smoking, which he promised to do. One morning, when he was hooked up to oxygen and drinking, he absent-mindedly lit up a cigarette. What a tragedy he created! The tank blew up and caught fire, and sadly, so did he. He managed to put out the flames and call 911 for help before the fire spread too badly. He was admitted to Sunnybrook Hospital with severe burns and died two weeks later.

Andrea always held a guarded affection for her father, and I could see the terrible pain in her eyes when he died. And in some strange way, part of me died with him too. Rick had very sadly left this world the same way he lived in it.

+++

About six months later, I was diagnosed with breast cancer. In a matter of hours after the terrifying news, I was thrust headlong into a whirlwind of doctor appointments, consultations, biopsies, scans, and X-rays. Through waves of gut-wrenching vulnerability, I felt my world closing in and choking the life right out of me. More than ever, I needed to be brave. Before surgery, there were many things to consider and decisions to be made. I was often overwhelmed and exhausted, just when I needed to keep my wits about me. I had my daughter or my husband with me for all medical discussions to take notes and keep me grounded.

By this time, I'd lived with lupus for about twenty-five years. It was mostly under control, but I still couldn't go in the sun because the UV rays would trigger an immune response, sending the illness into high gear. Therefore, although my cancer was a small nodule found in one breast, a lumpectomy was not an option for me because that type of surgery is followed by radiation. I was worried I wouldn't be able to tolerate the radiation treatment due to my condition. My surgeon couldn't definitively say if it was safe for me. It was my choice to make, so I chose not to go that route. Mastectomy was my next option, and despite the fact that I had cancer in only one breast, I knew from the start that I wanted both breasts removed.

Facing a mastectomy and never having had any major surgery in my life was very scary. I was sixty-nine years old and used to taking homeopathic remedies and natural healing methods to maintain my health. I can't tolerate chemical medications of any kind, and I knew the surgery would take its toll on my body. But with my family's full support, I was going for a bilateral mastectomy.

I had two reasons for making my decision. First, I couldn't imagine going through all this for a single mastectomy, followed up by ongoing mammograms on the other breast, only to go through it all over again if cancer was detected again in the future. The second reason was related to my self-esteem and sense of balance. The idea of being left with one large lopsided D-cup breast while the other side was flat disturbed my sense of order and well-being. Plus, I would be faced with the never-ending challenge of matching the flat side with a comfortable prosthesis.

I've always heard that it's a woman's choice when it comes to breast cancer options. But for me, getting my treatment choice wasn't easy. I was determined to do things my way, and I took up the challenge of convincing my doctors. My surgeon strongly argued against the double mastectomy because of the added risk, and while I could understand his need for caution, I persisted. He finally agreed to do the bilateral surgery, but only if I could get my family doctor onside. She initially argued against it, but after forcefully presenting my case, I eventually convinced her that removing both breasts was the right choice for me.

The day before my surgery, Andrea took me out for lunch. Afterwards, we sat in the parking lot, and I talked to her about the life we'd been through together and the enormity of my love for her and Farrell. Facing serious surgery and my own mortality, I talked to her about the details of my will and how best to deal with Bob if he found himself alone. It was an enormous burden I was placing on her, but I felt it necessary to tell her these things while I could. My fear of what was ahead loomed large, and I was more worried about how a bad ending for me would affect all of them. It was a comfort to say everything I needed to say in that moment as she held me in her arms. I had raised a strong young woman, and for that I was grateful.

The next morning, Andrea came to the hospital with me because Bob's back was in bad shape, and he could barely move. I could see the deep worry lines in his face, and his eyes reflected the regret he felt at not being able to come with me. But all I needed from him was one of his big bear hugs to take with me.

The scariest thing was the needle they injected directly into my nipples to administer the dye a few hours before surgery. The mere thought of it curled my toes. But I survived the nipple trauma, and two hours later, I said goodbye to my set of D cups and entered the operating room for a bilateral mastectomy.

✦✦✦

It was difficult to come to terms with the cancer label and my new image in the mirror. But I knew that, ultimately, getting well was up to me. I found meditation and belly breathing exercises invaluable tools during my post-surgery period. Bob's love and support went a long way to getting me through the worst of it. It was a long while before I was comfortable looking at my new body and even longer for me to show my husband.

The next big decision came a few weeks after surgery when I visited the oncologist. I was terrified at the prospect of needing chemotherapy or follow-up drug treatment. I couldn't imagine how my body would react to such toxic chemicals. I was relieved when the oncologist told me the surgery had successfully removed all the cancer and no chemo or radiation would be needed. Although my risk rate was very low for the cancer to return, my oncologist recommended I take a drug used as a post-cancer therapy. But after reading the frightening potential side effects, which included blood clots, strokes, uterine cancer, nausea, rashes, and eye problems, I declined. I'd take my chances without the drugs.

I know this isn't everyone's breast cancer story. I was fortunate to be able to choose not to take any ongoing drug treatment. I loved the comfort of "going flat" with the option of wearing a prosthesis only when I felt like it. Farrell, a typical kid, told me she couldn't wait for us to get back in pool. She always said it was my big boobs that allowed me to out-float her in the water. My granddaughter was sure I would sink to the bottom without them, and she wanted to be there to see that.

✦✦✦

When it was all over and I was feeling healthy again, I had a lot to say about what I went through. There were many issues that none of my medical team had prepared me for, which took me by surprise. I wrote an article about what I'd experienced and made several suggestions for other women who would face the same challenges. It was entitled "Flat and Fabulous" and has been published on several cancer-related websites around the world.

I don't take for granted how fortunate I've been. This was simply my cancer story, and I got my life back. For me, it was all about choice, asking the right questions, and being diligent in gathering the facts to weigh my options. A bold attitude didn't hurt either. If I'd made other choices or allowed the doctors to choose for me, my experience might have been completely different. I will forever remember my teenage experience with Dr. White and his prescribed concoction of uppers and downers. I still don't trust doctors to always know what's best for me. I have never been a one-size-fits-all kinda gal.

+++

Before and after this episode with cancer, I was busy writing more children's books. I didn't want to go through the never-ending rejection process inherent in a writer's life, so I formed Press Here to Start Publishing to publish them myself. I hired a proofreader, two illustrators, a book designer, and a printing company to complete my book projects. I was still doing workshops and readings at Farrell's school, so I engaged the kids to help me decide on the titles and cover pictures. More than two hundred children and their teachers were included in the selection process, and I found the whole exercise exhilarating. I went on to publish three books.

By that time, Farrell and I had spent many hours journaling together and talking about books and writing. Every year, I held creative writing contests for all the students in grades 4 to 6 at her school. It was a lot of fun, and Farrell helped me review all the entries and pick the winners. I had an arrangement with the *Oakville Beaver* newspaper to publish the best story. It became a highlight of the year for the students, especially the winner, who was proud to become a published author. I bought small gifts for all first-, second-, and third-place entries.

Doing all these things with Farrell was gratifying on so many levels. I was spending time with her as I never had with my own daughter. Maybe now that Andrea was a working mother busy building her career, she might better understand my motivations for focusing so much time on my work. Andrea and Sean were amazing parents to Farrell. We all did what we could to surround her with the best of all possible worlds, committed to keeping Farrell's fire burning brightly.

CHAPTER 21

Uphill Battles and MAID

By 2016, after publishing seven books for children, I decided to take a break from writing for a while. Bob needed more of my time because of his growing mobility issues. He was slowing down and would be eighty on his next birthday. He didn't look much like Tom Selleck anymore with a growing potbelly, balding head, and being hunched over a walker most of the time. But he could always make me laugh, and when he smiled with those dimples, he was still movie-star handsome to me.

Bob was a trooper when it came to his granddaughter. He often picked Farrell up at her daily taekwondo lessons after school. We were all so proud of her when she achieved her second-degree black belt at eleven years old. He was there every year on grandparents' day to deliver a unique presentation to Farrell's class. He beamed when her name was even mentioned and treasured every minute he spent with her. All things considered, life was feeling pretty good.

Then another tragedy struck when Bob was diagnosed with bladder cancer.

✦✦✦

We plunged into turmoil once again as our lives filled with doctors' appointments and tests. Bob needed to see a urologist and an oncologist at the cancer clinic at Credit Valley Hospital in Mississauga. We both found it exhausting to make the trip there and back several times a week. The hospital was huge, and it was tiring for Bob to get around with a walker. He was also twice my size and weight, so I found it a struggle to push him in a wheelchair.

The doctors started a steady treatment of BCG injections into his bladder; BCG, a live tuberculosis bacterium, had good reports in destroying cancer cells. It was potentially infectious to others, so during the treatments we needed to use separate bathrooms for safety reasons, and we used bleach to scour the toilet he used. He went through a year of those treatments, supplemented by a few surgeries to scrape the cancer cells. But each time, the malignancy grew back bigger and stronger while it metastasized and spread.

Estelle and Maureen stayed in touch with me every day during that time, and it meant so much to me to have my sisters in my life. Estelle came from Ottawa for a couple of visits, which helped both Bob and me feel more relaxed. She always had a smile, seamlessly helped with household chores, and kept things light. There was a sense of calm and comfort about this beautiful woman that was contagious.

+++

Over the months that followed, Bob slowly got weaker and couldn't go very far from home. He self-catheterized several times a day and wore diapers, which was devastating for him. He was becoming more and more dependent on me as his caregiver while he longed for his younger, healthier days and the freedom he once had. He cried a lot, and it broke my heart to see him in such anguish.

Bob missed his fishing days and was sad knowing that part of his life was gone for good. He watched angler shows on TV and longed to be out on the water. We looked at pictures and reminisced about the bonefishing we did together in the mangrove flats of Belize when I could still go in the sun. He especially enjoyed the fishing he did in Alberta, Alaska, and Yukon. On some of those trips, he used a belly boat, a large donut-shaped float tube with a suspended seat and holes for his legs. He wore flippers and kicked his way around the open water while he was fly fishing from the float tube. Sadly those days were gone, but thankfully the memories still brought him joy.

+++

We were struggling to keep up with the demands of the disease when tragedy struck again. My beloved sister Estelle died.

It all happened so fast. Estelle saw her doctor in February because she had back pain and was having trouble urinating. Tests revealed she was full of cancer: it was in her brain, stomach, liver, breasts, spleen, lungs, bowels, and even in her spine. Just like that. I felt like I was dreaming when her daughter Andi called to tell me the devastating news. Doctors had given her four months tops. Estelle left us two months later in April at only sixty-nine years old.

I visited my sister in the hospital the day before she passed. We knew she had only hours to live, and it was a painful car ride from Oakville to Ottawa. Bob was driving, and I developed a full-on anxiety attack. We stopped at a hospital along the way, and when they confirmed it wasn't my heart, we continued on.

When we arrived at her hospital room to say our goodbyes, Estelle's family was there, and John was feeding her ice chips from a spoon. I had a few minutes alone with her, and as I held her hand, I broke down, saying "How am I going to live without you?" I couldn't hold back the sorrow that was crushing my heart.

She looked at me and squeezed my hand. "I know," she said weakly. "But look at me. I'm hooked up to all these tubes, and I need morphine every few minutes for the pain. I can't live like this. It's time."

Estelle and I had been tightly braided into each other's lives for so long, I couldn't see my life without her in it. I loved everything about my sister: her soft diplomatic nature, her infectious laughter, her generosity, and her big expressive brown eyes. Estelle was the most beautiful soul I knew. I cried all the way back to Oakville, deep guttural sobs of pain and despair. She died the next day with her immediate family around her.

When I lost Estelle, my heart hurt so much I was sure I'd never recover. I'd always felt I could get through anything with my sister. But when she died, I had thoughts of wanting to die too; I needed to be with her. My whole life had been with her. It was like a nightmare, and I couldn't wake up. But Bob needed me, so I pushed my way through the grief and buried my emotions. I buckled down and knew my days with Bob could be limited. I was grateful for every minute we had, even if all we did was sit in the same room together.

+++

In August 2018, we attended an appointment with Bob's oncologist. We went into the meeting with a list of questions about next steps. The doctor told us that his cancer had spread, and there were no more treatments or surgeries that could help him. Our options had run out, and he gave him a year at most.

We left the hospital in a daze, but Bob insisted he was okay to drive home. He was a bit slow making a right turn on a red light, and an old red car behind us leaned on the horn without letting up. After we made the turn, two young men in the same red, rusted-out Chevy pulled up beside us and began screaming obscenities out the window, mostly about how old people "should get off the f***ing road." They kept this up for about ten minutes, following inches behind on our bumper or pulling up beside us as they continued to hang out of the car and curse through the open window. Bob and I were silent, held our breaths, and looked straight ahead. They eventually lost interest and turned down a side street.

It would have been a cruel encounter at any time but was especially upsetting after the appointment we'd just had. Bob was even more upset than I because he'd felt helpless to defend us if the young men had gotten violent. To Bob, it was another reminder of how impotent his life had become.

✦✦✦

Bob and I had to face the harsh reality that the end was coming. I'd watch him sleeping in his chair wrapped in a red heated blanket, and I knew I was slowly losing him in small, heartbreaking pieces. He began to sleep more and eat less.

I soon started to experience severe panic attacks, with heart palpitations and moments of near blacking out. There was nothing doctors could do except prescribe relaxants, which I resisted taking. I needed to be awake and in charge to take care of Bob. I coped well enough with the cooking, cleaning, and caregiving I did every day. But when I allowed myself to rest or think of the future, my body would respond with episodes of atrial fibrillation and vertigo. Once again, I had arrived at a stage of my life without any idea how to get through it. I took one day at a time, put one foot in front of the other, and prayed I would find my way.

Ever since that first poem I wrote when my daughter was born, I've used writing as a release valve on my emotions — like opening a steam vent on a pressure cooker. Several years before, I'd started a blog called *Boomerrantz*, where I posted mostly humorous reflections and unbridled ranting on the adventures and misadventures of everyday life. In September 2018, I was taking Bob for daily palliative radiation treatments in an attempt to slow the cancer down. I took to my blog to post a more serious and uncharacteristic piece about how I was feeling.

Do You Know This Woman? (September 17, 2018)

She could be someone you know; she's not alone in this situation. But this is her story. Taking care of her husband is an all-consuming task every day, all day, all the time. Some days she feels like she's disappearing. But then she looks in the mirror and she's still there; still breathing, still brushing her teeth, still putting on her eyeliner. She feels like she's being carried along in a rapid current of water. She makes endless lists of things that need to be done but forgets to shower sometimes. She knows he needs her. She knows his illness is terminal.

With every cell that dies inside of him, a little bit of her dies too. But she can still make him smile, and he still has a few good jokes to make her laugh. She tried to dance for him a few weeks ago to cheer him up. It was a Saturday morning after he had come home from a hospital stay. She jiggled her hips to the dance of the seven tea towels across the kitchen, but it didn't end well. She tripped and launched herself into a head-dive into the next room. Yes, her heart was in the right place, but then it was in the wrong place … under the dining room table. She had fallen and she couldn't get up.

She's been with him for over four decades. His every mood and movement is bred in the bone. His 83rd birthday was last week, and they spent it in the hospital.

Her sister's delicious chicken soup helps a lot and lulls her back into her childhood, a nice respite for a while. Her daughter's cooking frenzy in the kitchen is a comfort of the heart. And the care and kindness offered up by friends and family is always there. She finds it hard to know how to ask for help. She's flummoxed about the dilemma of what they can do to make this easier. It's never going to be easy. But she finally learns that getting caregiving help at home is not about him, it's about her.

After he's in bed, she sits in the living room and listens to the quiet. She thinks about him singing "Old Man River" at a dinner party many years ago. Just two Halloweens past, he donned a cowboy hat and tied a string of toast around his neck. He told everyone at the party he was a toasted western.

Some days she thinks she's doing God's work. Some days she thinks she's failing at living up to the task. But every day, she uses her binoculars to find the light at the end of the cancer.

He always lived large in everything he did. He taught her how to do that. And now she has to teach him how to live small, and she's not sure she can. But she tries to live small with him so they can learn together. Every day, a little bit more of him retreats, and every day she watches him disintegrate. There's always more hope and more prayers, but there's always more reality than either of them wants to face.

So if you know this woman, all she needs from you is a hug. I hear she collects them and periodically leaps into the pile to be surrounded by your good wishes, while she works at recharging her batteries. We can do this, she tells herself. This too shall pass ...

✦✦✦

The oncologist and our family doctor approved Bob for palliative services, which would give him more care at home. He struggled with showering and dressing himself and could no longer do any cooking or drive a car. His list of medications was complex. The visiting nurses and doctors helped to prescribe what he needed to make him comfortable, and I hired private caregivers to help me with the rest.

Bob lost interest in going anywhere out of our condo. He fell a couple of times getting out of his chair, and with his weight, I struggled to help him up. Even though he wore incontinence underwear, he had occasional accidents. He would look at me with such sadness and tell me how sorry he was that I had to clean up his messes. I assured him over and over that I wanted to do everything I could to keep him home with me for as long as possible.

✦✦✦

Then one day, Bob decided he'd had enough of the pain, the blood, the endless supply of diapers, and the confinement.

"I've outlived my mother, my father, my sister, and most of my best friends. I think it's time for me to join them," he said. I didn't know what to say.

Bob's dad died from bladder cancer in his sixties. That was always on his mind because he had the same type of disease as his father. His sister Carole was younger than Bob by fifteen years. Sadly, she died at sixty-one after a horrific battle with mouth cancer where the surgeons removed part of her face in an attempt to save her. His mother lived to ninety-seven and spent her final years confined to a room in a nursing home.

"God has forgotten me," she would repeat over and over, on every visit we made.

Most of Bob's fishing buddies were gone, and he'd given a eulogy just the year before for another good friend. After witnessing so many people in his life die, Bob always told me there was a look he could see in people's eyes when they were close to death. He wasn't a particularly intuitive man, but he swore this was something he could see. Bob said he felt an overwhelming sadness that his life was at an end, and he started talking about ways to die by suicide.

+++

Not knowing where to turn with this frightening information, I discussed it with my daughter, who told me about the MAID program, medical assistance in dying. This is a doctor-assisted suicide for qualifying patients, approved in Ontario in 2017. Bob and I studied the information, and he decided that was what he wanted to do. After reviewing all the facts and going through the required doctor visits, counselling sessions, and medical forms, Bob was approved for MAID in October 2018. He was more determined than ever to choose a date and proceed. The only catch was that he had to be capable of giving consent right up to the time of injection. In other words, he could not give his instructions in advance. This worried him a lot because he'd already had two TIAs (small strokes) and was afraid he might have a more serious one and lose his window of consent.

He chose November, just a month away, as the time for him to die. It felt surreal to me. On the one hand, I was thankful we were no longer discussing suicide. But we were still talking about his death. While I was frightened and confused, I also felt a sense of relief that there would be an end to this for both of us. Andrea took a sabbatical from her job, and we sadly began making preparations for that date. But once again, something intervened.

+++

I'd been having occasional spasms in my right groin for a couple of years. My orthopaedic surgeon had told me I needed a hip replacement, but I'd been putting it off to take care of Bob. My plan was to get the surgery done after this ordeal was over. But in October, I experienced a spasm so severe I couldn't walk for days. The surgeon knew my situation with Bob in palliative care at home and offered to fit me in right away to do the replacement. I resisted strongly because the timing was way off. I didn't think I could handle one more thing! I was already on maximum overload.

Bob begged me to proceed and said he would delay the MAID date until I'd recovered. He wanted me to get the surgery over with while he was still with me, saying I would have enough to deal with afterwards. I agreed to have my hip replacement surgery a week later. The operation was a success, and I hired full-time nursing care for both of us to get through the first couple of weeks. Afterwards, I kept a nurse on for a few hours every day to help me with Bob. I recuperated quickly, and I was soon walking without a cane.

◆◆◆

As my role in Bob's life increasingly changed from wife to full-time caregiver, I missed the intimacy we once had and knew that part of my life was gone. But he remained affectionate, holding my hand, and hugging me more than usual, telling me he loved me several times a day. I found myself detaching from my emotions to concentrate on what he needed. I told myself that there would be time to deal with my own emotional state when all this was over. I slept on alert, with one ear focused on his every sound and movement beside me during the night. He often needed pills or juice or ice to ease the pain.

Out-of-town family came to say their goodbyes, a difficult thing to do for everyone. My sister, Maureen, and her husband, Dave, hurried the sale of their Florida condo so that they could be back in time to see Bob one last time. He struggled to stay awake and upbeat during everyone's short visits, but he then would collapse into bed exhausted when they left.

He began sleeping even more and took myriad pills to keep comfortable. Sometimes, I would sit and watch him sleep, thankful for the storm that nearly capsized our boat in the Grenadines. In the end, that frightening experience and a novena made in the height of terror saved my marriage and allowed me forty-two wonderful years with this man of mine. It's strange how very bad things can become very good things in the end. We just don't know it at the time.

◆◆◆

Bob knew Christmas was my favourite time of year, so he vowed to make it through his last holiday with us. Andrea had picked up the gauntlet of cooking all holiday dinners at her house after we moved to Oakville. Her house was much bigger than my condo. But that Christmas, she and her family moved the turkey dinner to our dining room, and Bob managed to get to the table to take his seat in his usual spot. He even made his favourite old Victorian toast:

"Here's a toast to them as we love,
And a toast to them as loves us.
And here's to them, who loves them,
Who loves those, who loves those,
Who loves them, that loves us.
Only the sober can say it and only the drunk can understand it.
Merry Christmas one and all!"

That Christmas Day, Bob sat at one end of the table and I sat at the other, with everyone else sandwiched in on the sides. My niece Jessica was one of Bob's favourite people, and she joined us that year as well. At one point, I glanced down the table at Bob to take a picture and I saw it — the "death look" he always talked about. It took my breath away. There was a vacancy in his eyes that chilled me; the spark that always matched his dimples was gone. I don't think I'll ever forget that look. I wasn't sure my husband was even in there anymore. I fought back the tears and deleted the picture from my phone.

We spent Christmas evening in the living room singing songs accompanied by Sean on the guitar. Andrea and Jessica got carried away with a crazy duo they concocted, and we were all in hysterics. Bob sat in his recliner surrounded by his family, grinning at the shenanigans going on. It was the perfect last Christmas.

The next hurdle was our wedding anniversary on New Year's Eve. Bob was determined that we would spend that day together. Bob and I could never understand why anyone would go to bed before midnight on New Year's Eve. It's such a magical time, when one year ends and another begins. The meaning for us that night was very different from the many years before. It would be the end of something, not the beginning. We watched the ball drop in Times Square and had a sip of twenty-year-old

Scotch. We didn't cry. We held back our sorrow and simply thanked each other for the wonderful life we'd shared.

Once the holidays were past, Bob was ready to go. He teared up a lot when he was alone, and sometimes I would wake up in the middle of the night with him sobbing beside me. He told me over and over again that he didn't want to leave me. All I could do was hold him. Finally, on January 7, 2019, he said he was ready to die and wanted the MAID procedure to go ahead the next day. He could barely get out of bed by then and couldn't even look at the food he'd once loved. Bob was always a powerfully built man with a well-muscled body and super strength. It upset him to watch his arms wasting away into sagging wrinkled skin. Now, he was unable to sit up in bed. It broke my heart to see the sorrow in his eyes because he was so helpless, and I knew he couldn't live like that anymore. Some days, I felt like I was dying right alongside him. With my hands shaking and my heart pounding, I did as he asked and got on the telephone with the MAID team. Andrea and I made all the arrangements for the next day with attention to detail like we were planning a party. I was grateful that Bob had the right to choose his death and leave all that suffering behind. And I was thankful he could be at home in his own bed to say goodbye. But he was going to die all the same.

We had one more night together, and we didn't spend it sleeping. We lay side by side, and Bob, being Bob, made me promise to check all his old lottery tickets for a winner before throwing them out. Then he went over some last-minute financial directions to ensure I'd be okay. We held many separate accounts because of the perks we got from our CIBC and Royal Bank careers. Before he got too sick, he had organized everything for me and had already written down where his accounts were and the contacts involved.

Then I broke the tension a bit by reminding him of something that happened about five years into our relationship. We were at home watching Woody Allen's *Annie Hall*, snuggled up with a glass of wine. At one point, Alvy had his first dinner date with Annie, and he stopped on the sidewalk to say, "You know, we've never kissed before and I'll never know when to make the right move. So, we'll kiss now, we'll get it over with and then we'll go eat."

My jaw had dropped when I heard that dialogue, and I turned to look at Bob, who was red-faced and grinning like a Cheshire cat. "You bugger!" I said. "You used those exact lines from the movie on our first date."

"I thought it was rather clever," he said sheepishly. "And it worked like a charm, didn't it?"

We both laughed at the memory. "You were smooth," I told him.

Then we talked about our many travels together, and that put a bit of energy back in his voice. It was always such a big part of our life. We enjoyed our Caribbean vacations and the cruises we'd been on, but we both loved the more adventurous memories the most.

We talked about riding the Shinkansen bullet train in Japan at 230 kilometres per hour, climbing the Great Wall of China, watching a bullfight in Portugal, seeing the midnight sun in Whitehorse, Yukon, air-boating through the alligator swamps of the Everglades, walking the trails through hot springs and gushing geysers in Yellowstone National Park, riding the water taxis in Thailand through rivers of floating hyacinths, exploring the streets of Seoul and Beijing, and sitting under a waterfall in a Hawaiian rainforest. These shared memories ran deep in our relationship, and Bob finished with a sigh. "I guess I've had a good life." With that, we eased into quiet gratitude. Throughout our reminiscing, nurses came in and out of the bedroom to reinsert the IV that kept falling out of his arm. Andrea slept in the guest room, and I was grateful she was nearby.

It was a surreal night, as if we were being crushed in a vise. I was lost, empty inside, and terrified. I was going to be a widow, and I was already starting to feel frightened and abandoned. My world was cracking, and I was helpless to stop it. For now, Bob and I needed to hang on and do this together. I'd convinced myself I was ready to face my husband's death, but I knew nothing of the impact it would have on me.

♦♦♦

When morning came, a special palliative care nurse arrived to help us through the day. She was great with Bob and gave the rest of us comfort in knowing she was there for anything we needed. The MAID doctor would arrive with her team at three in the afternoon to do the procedure.

Sean had recently converted Bob's old movie reels into a CD he could watch on my laptop. One by one, we went into the bedroom and sat with him to watch old footage of Bob as a young boy with his family and happy memories of several fishing trips he took with his buddies. He sobbed every time he went through the pictures, and when I asked if it was too upsetting, he told me he found it comforting to see his family and old friends again.

The MAID doctor had already told Bob he could choose what he wanted to wear for the procedure. She said some people got all dressed up like they were going to a wedding. Bob made me laugh every day we were together even when he was sick. It was no different on the day he died. That morning, when the nurse was getting him washed and dressed, she asked him what he wanted to wear.

He said curtly, "Well, I'm certainly not getting into a suit and tie, if that's what you mean." I suggested he simply wear his Depends and a T-shirt so he would be comfortable in bed.

He looked me square in the eye and said, "I'm NOT going out of this world in a diaper! Get me my Marvel Comics underwear." Pure Bob, right to the end. He was getting ready to die accompanied by a colourful cast of brave superheroes.

♦♦♦

An hour before the procedure, Andrea, Sean, and Farrell all piled on the big four-poster king-sized bed with Bob and me, and we had a picnic prepared by the nurse. We had Brie cheese, crackers, grapes, strawberries, and glasses of Dom Pérignon. We all toasted Bob and his life while the attending nurse took pictures in our bedroom. I still look at those pictures from time to time when I'm missing him. Bob is smiling in all of them, happy and at peace surrounded by his family in his final moments.

When the MAID team arrived, Andrea, Sean, and Farrell came into the bedroom one by one to say goodbye. It was heartbreaking for all of us, especially for Andrea who said goodbye to the stepfather who loved her as if she were his own. It was devastating to see how Farrell was shaken to the core. She was sixteen, and this was her first experience with death, and it was with her beloved Poppy. She hugged him and said goodbye, and then turned at the door and came back in the room bawling to do it all over again.

Bob had written Farrell a letter to read after he was gone. He also dictated letters to me for Andrea and Sean with a few last words for each of them. I didn't need a letter; we'd had the beautiful luxury of saying everything we needed to say. We knew our story was finished and the goodbyes hurt but needed to be said. In those final moments, I could see he was more relaxed than he'd been for many months. He looked at peace with his decision, and he was ready.

Bob didn't want to put his daughter and granddaughter through the trauma of watching him die, so he wanted only me present. The doctor knelt on the bed beside him, and I sat in a chair near his head, holding his hand while she prepared the needle. She asked for his final consent, which he gave, and asked if we had anything more to say before she proceeded.

Bob closed his eyes and squeezed my hand. "I love you so much," he said. Tears flowed down his face.

"Thanks for a wonderful life," I told him. "Give Estelle a hug for me."

I remember the warmth of his hand in mine and how he tensed when the doctor injected his arm. I felt his grip tighten, as if he were trying to hang on or take me with him. When she gave Bob the second injection, his hand softened and went slack in mine. Then she administered the final needle. I watched as the rhythmic pulse in his neck slowly faded away and the heart that kept him alive for eighty-three years stopped beating. My Bob was still lying there, but he was gone.

I held his hand long after the final moments passed, and the medical team had left the building. Bob still felt warm and looked like he was sleeping. I felt numb, as if I were drifting through a dream. Then the undertakers from the crematorium arrived and suggested to my daughter that I move to another room.

Bob's ordeal was over.

CHAPTER 22

Fallout

The day after I watched my husband die, my brain shut down. I was sitting with my son-in-law in the den, and my daughter was on the phone in the kitchen. Sean casually mentioned that I might like to go and stay with my sister in Cobourg for a while.

"Why would I do that?" I asked him.

"You know, to help you get through this," Sean said cautiously.

"Get through what?"

"Ummm, you know, Bob's death and everything. You might need your sister for a while."

"Bob died?" I screamed at him. "When? Where the hell was I? Why don't I know this?"

He frantically called for my daughter and dialled 911. When the ambulance arrived and the paramedic said, "I understand you lost your husband yesterday," I became very distraught all over again.

"My husband died?" I repeated. I wanted to know when it happened and why I wasn't there. Every time they told me, it brought on a fresh wave of panic. I was stuck in a loop and couldn't remember anything about Bob's death.

My daughter knelt beside me and gently took me through the events of the day before. She showed me pictures of the picnic we had on the bed with Bob. Andrea spoke very softly and walked me through each detail as the paramedics looked on. Slowly my memory started to come back, but it was like connecting distorted images through a fog.

The paramedics said I'd developed temporary amnesia, common in cases of trauma. They added that it wasn't serious unless it continued to happen, which it never did again. Although it didn't last long, it was a surreal experience.

+++

The next day, my daughter and I went to the crematorium to make arrangements. My sister, Maureen, and her husband, Dave, met us there to take me back to Cobourg with them. It was their daughter Jessica's house, but they were staying with her that winter after selling their Florida condo to rush home to see Bob. When Andrea did the hand-off, I could see the relief in her eyes. She'd been through hell right alongside me and hadn't time to start her own grieving. My daughter lost her father, her godmother, and her stepfather in such a short period of time.

After two years of constant worry and intense caregiving, I was empty. I had nothing left. I felt as fragile as the touch-me-not wildflowers I loved as a child. My brain was in sleep mode as I floated through the hours. Maureen and Dave made all the decisions about what to eat, where to go, and when to rest. Jessica watched me closely and distracted me with conversations about books and school shenanigans. My niece was an elementary school principal, so she always had some excellent stories to tell. I felt a welcome numbness in my escape while being well loved and cared for.

I watched TV with them every night, got dressed when they told me we were going out, and slept wrapped in Bob's red blanket. My sister cooked delicious meals, but I was nauseous all the time, so it was hard to eat anything. As Maureen's older sister by nine years, I've always felt very protective of her. She seemed more fragile than Estelle and me. But suddenly, I saw the strength that had always been there. I gave in to her care and feeding like a child, and she made me feel safe and loved. Thankfully, she held onto me with an iron grip and stopped me from floating away.

On one of those occasions when I was beginning to feel a bit better, we went to a local diner for a breakfast of bacon and eggs. Dave took out the jam holder and chose a packet of marmalade. As I watched him spread it on his toast, I shocked everyone, including myself, by breaking out into uncontrollable sobbing. Bob loved marmalade. I was inconsolable for the rest of the day.

After a couple of weeks at Jessica's, I began to feel stronger and ready to go home. Well, not exactly ready, but I knew it was time.

+++

The part that haunted me most was that Bob chose to die, and I helped with his decision. That being said, I support the MAID program and am grateful that my husband had this option available to him. It gave him a sense of control, and he was at peace with his decision. It also gave us time to talk, do some financial planning, and say our goodbyes. I thought I was ready for the days that would follow his death. I thought I would feel relief, and yes maybe even a bit of freedom. But none of those things happened. While the MAID team did a good job preparing both of us for his dying, it did not prepare me for his death or the intense emotional trauma I experienced in watching him die.

For months before his final hour, we had doctors, nurses, caseworkers, counsellors, homecare workers, family, and friends coming and going all day. But everything came to a screeching halt when he died and everyone left. They all simply returned to the same world they woke up to that morning. My world had frayed at the edges, and then it fell apart.

My feelings of guilt and self-doubt went into overdrive. Did I do the right thing? Should I have asked him to stay? Did he die too soon? Did he feel rushed in deciding the date? All of the "what ifs" were in an endless loop that tortured me every day. I wondered if my last memory of watching him die and the images of that vein in his neck would ever go away.

I needed help but none was available. I contacted the service agency that facilitated MAID and asked for a support group. I was told there wasn't one specific for MAID survivors because of the newness of the program. There was a general bereavement group, but because they cohort the group, I would not be eligible to join until nine months after his death. I was grateful to have my family during that time, but I still felt abandoned and alone as I continued in crisis.

Part Six (2019–2023)

We must be willing to get rid of the life we had planned, so as to have the life that is waiting for us. The old skin has to be shed before the new one can come.

— Joseph Campbell

CHAPTER 23

Message in a Bottle

Four months after Bob's death, I was lying on a pier near my home, shivering in the cold with a spider crawling up my pant leg. The angry waves echoed the continual pounding and never-ending ache in my chest. I tried to find comfort from the water, but even the Lake Ontario gods had forsaken me. Feeling smothered in despair, I got up and made my way back to the emptiness of my condo.

Whenever I opened the door to my unit, Bob's voice didn't greet me as it had for so many years. There were no cooking smells coming from the kitchen, and the only sound was CNN blasting away on the TV in the den. I headed to the shower and let the hot water pour over my body until I stopped shaking. Then I wrapped myself in Bob's old grey cardigan and settled down in his lift chair with a cup of Bengal Spice tea. Another endless night stretched out in front of me, like empty arms reaching into the darkness.

+++

The next day, I got on with a secret project I'd started recently. Fifteen little glass bottles with cork stoppers were lined up in front of me along with an equal number of one-inch paper strips. I wrote uplifting or humorous quotes on each one, words to brighten someone's day. Then I rolled them up tightly into a little scroll, wrote the word "Message" on the side, and stuffed one into each bottle. After pushing in the corks, I tied bright green ribbons around the necks of the bottles and glued a sparkly jewel on the tops.

I was inspired to create these little bottles when I visited my friend Veronica in Cobourg after Bob died. She was recovering from multiple myeloma, and during her healing, she began painting small rocks with colourful designs. She would leave them in public places around the town. She told me it lifted her spirits to reach out and touch people in that way. I was so intrigued I returned home and began my own version of her project. I placed little anonymous inspirational messages into small bottles and left them scattered around my neighbourhood, as Veronica had done with her rocks.

⬥⬥⬥

It was late afternoon and I needed to get out, so I grabbed my jacket and dropped the fifteen little bottles into my purse. As I walked down to the garage, my shoulders ached, and my back felt like I was carrying a sack of turnips.

I drove to the Woodside Branch of the Oakville Public Library, which was only a few minutes away. Since I'd started my project, I'd taken my little bottles to places like shopping malls, movie theatres, and various parks and restaurants. The trick was to secretly leave the bottles in random places.

When I reached the library, I cased the place first, wandering between the rows of books. When no one was around, I looked for spaces on the shelves where I could put my bottles for people to find. I placed them all, dropping the last two bottles in the return slot and in the pocket of a man's coat slung over a chair.

Feeling a bit giddy from the covert nature of what I was doing, I left the library and headed for the parking lot. My smiling reflection in the car window looked back at me as I reached to open the door. "You're one weird old lady," I told myself.

I wondered if any of the people I met would find my messages. I knew they wouldn't mean something to everyone. But to me, words had a life of their own, like a musical note or a song. What if I made just one person feel happy or have a new thought about life in general? I couldn't control how numb I felt, but maybe I could make another person feel something. I loved the mystery of it all. Leaving my bottles always gave me a bit of colour in my otherwise black and white world. At least it took my mind away from the never-ending emptiness at home.

Was my bottle project a serious cry for help, a longing for connection to the world around me in some small way? I was on a mission without ever knowing if what I was doing made a difference to anyone but me.

I felt a strange sense of joy from knowing that nearly five hundred pieces of me were out there making their way into people's lives. It helped me to feel a tangible connection to something bigger in the midst of my loneliness that sometimes swallowed me up. And on some level, maybe I was hoping for a divine message of intervention that would heal my life, in the same way I dreamed my messages would impact the people who found them.

+++

When I returned home, the worst thing to endure was the emptiness of a home without a pulse. As I walked through the door, the quiet seemed to amplify into a deafening roar. I'd suffered from tinnitus for years, but now there were days when the bees in my head buzzed in four-part harmony. Some days, it was more like a chainsaw orchestra. Dinner times were hard. Bob loved to cook, and I missed his experiments with fancy new recipes from his Williams Sonoma cookbook and the spicy Mediterranean dishes he cooked in the tagine Andrea bought him one Christmas. As usual, CNN would be on the TV to keep me company. I did that a lot — listen to CNN with their endless supply of talking heads and breaking news. Grief had a way of screaming in the silence, so even the monotonous drone of commentators was a welcome diversion.

To make it through another dinner alone, I'd often grab my waterproof MP3 player and swimbuds (another epic gift from Bob) and head down to the pool. I was lifted into another softer world, as I floated effortlessly with my eyes closed, listening to beautiful music like "The Blue Danube." Alone in the deep end of the pool, I'd move my arms and legs in a hypnotic water-dance to the rhythm of the orchestra. Night after night, I found comfort in water as I always had; even if it was chlorinated pool water, it still worked.

When I'd return upstairs, my go-to meal was often a bowl of Campbell's Tomato soup and two slices of toasted raisin bread. As much as I wasn't interested in cooking, I was still battling intermittent bouts of nausea and didn't find many foods appealing. It reminded me of the stressful days after Andrea was born, when I existed on nothing but chocolate cake and grape pop.

+++

It was sad to feel so helpless and without direction. I could never have imagined how the strength I most admired in this powerful man would shrivel up with a disease that devoured his body. For years, I had leaned on Bob to give me the courage to stand straight and tall. But when he couldn't do it anymore, he needed to lean on me. I was his rock, his strength, his nursemaid, and his emotional walking stick. Then, in only two short years after diagnosis, he was gone, and any strength I had left went with him. Questions continued to pound away in my head. I needed to know if I did the right thing in helping him to die.

Despite my little bottles of joy, I was still battling a darkness that struck me at the slightest provocation: a B.B. King song, Bob's chair at the kitchen table where he read the newspaper with his breakfast, or a TV show we enjoyed watching together. It was especially difficult to see older couples walking together holding hands. Some days, the sadness was like a giant wave crashing over me, the current pushing me down. All of him was there with me, all the time. On one level, it was comforting to sense him near me, but I felt stuck, unable to move past the life we had. I was shrinking back into who I used to be, unable to trust myself to survive alone. While I tried to face my grief head-on, my biggest fears continued to stare back at me: fear of getting old, fear of getting sick, fear of falling and never getting up. I wondered how I would ever find my way to living a new life without my husband. I needed my dad's oilskin coat to protect me from the storm.

CHAPTER 24

Filling Empty Spaces

I had to take care of the estate business, and my work brain kicked into gear. As difficult as it was to give all the necessary notifications about Bob's death, it felt good to have something to focus on, and grief took a temporary back seat. I created a chart of items that needed attention, and those became my to-do list each day. A small sense of accomplishment and forward movement was a welcome relief. I found little moments of release from the anguish by keeping Bob close to me. Sometimes, I'd put on the silk scarf he gave me for my birthday, drink my tea from his favourite cup, or write with the beautiful emerald green pen he gave me when I published my first book.

My husband was the best gift-giver and always had unique ideas for each one of us in the family. He thought deeply about the gifts he gave; you might even say he could go a bit over the top. One year, Bob wrote to the Canadian Coast Guard in Parry Sound and obtained a copy of the construction plans for the Gereaux Island Lighthouse, which means so much to many generations of my family. He found a wood craftsman in our neighbourhood who could follow the plans to make an exact replica model. The artist built the lighthouse to the original design in every detail, finishing it in the iconic red and white painted exterior.

Bob presented it to me at Christmas that year, and to this day, I think it's the most loving gift I've ever received. For one of my birthdays, he had an artist do a watercolour of the Holy Family Church in Britt. I cherish the painting, which hangs in my bedroom today. To me, these gifts are a reminder of how deeply thoughtful Bob was and how much he truly loved me. I began to realize the depth of my grief was in direct proportion to the depth of the love I had for him.

◆◆◆

I talked to some women friends who'd lost their husbands, but I found it hard to relate to their stories because of the way Bob died.

I didn't know anyone who had experienced a MAID death. But still, they were widows, and I wanted to know how they moved on. Everyone's grief takes a different form, but what I was really searching for was hope that someday I'd find comfort in living alone. That was still my biggest challenge. Most of the women told me they never got used to it, and the loneliness never went away. Some quickly entered into new relationships to solve the problem, but that wasn't even remotely on my radar.

Would I ever feel comfortable on my own? Will the pain of losing him ever go away? Did I do the right thing helping him to die? I felt a desperate need to dig deep and get more control over my life. I'd once found the emotional strength to leave a bad marriage and drive across the Rockies to start a new life with my daughter. That was over four decades ago, and my inner warrior was buried pretty deep. I needed to coax her out and be that young woman in the lime green car again.

+++

In the weeks that followed, Andrea helped me clean out Bob's desk, his dressers, and his closets. The man was always messier than five teenagers!

A thoughtful friend of mine offered to make a quilt using patches from Bob's shirts. At the time, it saddened me to think of having a quilt like that, so I thanked her and declined. But looking back now, I wish I had such a lovely reminder of him. I kept one red checkered shirt that he loved to wear and tucked it into the back of my closet. I wanted to save his old grey cardigan to wrap around me, but all I could see when I looked at it was his suffering. So I let it go. We packed up multiple bags of clothing and a bunch of coats and shoes, which Andrea drove to the Salvation Army drop-off. I couldn't go with her and watch his belongings be left in a warehouse to be given away to strangers. Is this what our lives are reduced to in the end — remnants of a life packed into plastic garbage bags?

Regardless of my unease with the purging, Bob was gone whether or not I kept his belongings. I felt an urgent need to weed out things that made me feel sad to look at and replace them with something new, something that didn't remind me of Bob.

+++

In the months that followed, I softened the grieving process by distracting myself with shopping. Lots of shopping. First, I bought some new living room furniture, throwing out our matching wing chair recliners. We shared so many enjoyable years side by side in those chairs, but now it pained me every time I looked at them. Then, I remodelled the guest bedroom, bought several new pieces of art, and gave away the antique armoire circa 1860 Bob loved so much. I changed my old oak kitchen table and chairs, where he used to sit reading the paper, for a more compact black and white chrome set, reminiscent of the 1950s.

Everything I purchased was scaled down from what I had before. Due to Bob's size, all our furniture had been chosen to fit his weight and stature. Now, it was like I was trying to erase him from my memory. I moved his lift chair from the den where he spent his final months and put it in my bedroom. I offered it to my sister for her cottage but changed my mind at the last moment, unable to let it go. I felt lonely and sad at the thought of losing it.

Then, all the clothes shopping, shoe shopping, and spa treatments started. I became a woman possessed and determined to fill my days with distractions as I tried to reinvent myself and move on. I took my social calendar out of mothballs, got back in touch with friends, and became a woman who does lunch.

I was finding the weekends hard, so I asked three other women who also lived alone to join me for a card game one Saturday night. We became good friends and began meeting once a week. After caregiving for so long, I wasn't used to this new level of freedom and activity. Bob hadn't even been gone a full year, and I felt guilty for shopping, laughing, and having fun. But I pushed those thoughts away. Everything looked perfect; my condo looked fresh and new, I looked fresh and new, and my calendar was filling up with things to do. But something was blistering under the surface, and when it all came crashing down, I fell into another dark place.

+++

I felt myself fading away again and disconnecting from my friends and family. I cried more often and walked the floors through the night, looking out the windows from the emptiness of my condo. My nausea had returned. I couldn't eat, and I had no interest in seeing anyone.

As it turned out, I was fresh and new only on the outside. But on the inside, I was still in the same state of disrepair. While I'd kept myself busy from morning to night with diversions to fill the silence, the smothering sadness had been growing in my gut. I didn't want to stop missing Bob; I just wanted it to stop hurting so much.

I looked for something to fix me faster and joined a bereavement group for spouses. I was nervous about going, but after getting there and listening to other people's stories, I was comforted by our shared experiences. But after only a few meetings, I began sinking even deeper into that black abyss of grief. While I didn't want to believe it was the heavy sadness in the group that was causing my backward slide, I decided to leave the sessions. I've always been a receptor of the energy in my surroundings, so this wasn't too much of a surprise. I guess I inherited some of my mother's spidey senses.

It was a good decision to quit the bereavement group, and I saw a healing therapist for a few intense sessions. She worked me hard to face my fears instead of burying them. I realized that I'd been trying to go around my grief instead of going through it. Eventually, her therapies helped to dig me out of the dark hole I'd fallen back into. But not before I'd ruined all those spa facials with crying binges that went on for hours at a time. When I cried after hearing something that reminded me of Bob, Andrea would say, "Cry till you sigh, Mom." And that's what I did. I would just let 'er rip and have a good loud sobbing fest because I'd learned it was going to come out one way or another. Instead of running away from my pain, I finally slowed down and let it catch up to me.

✦✦✦

When the grief settled and I looked around my condo, I loved all the changes I'd made to make the place feel like my own. But I realized that perhaps I'd moved too quickly and didn't give my emotions a chance to have a say in the process. I wondered in retrospect if I should have given away Bob's beloved antique pine armoire, something he treasured. Maybe not, but it was with a dear friend who loved it and put it to good use, so I was okay with that. I'd like to think Bob would understand.

I sat remembering all that had happened since Bob left, and I was grateful to be feeling calmer and more peaceful. I was still coming to terms with things, but my thoughts were tempered with more confidence that I could find my way to living a new life alone.

CHAPTER 25

Boot Camp

In the months that followed, my daughter often left her family to eat dinner with me or sleep overnight. I'd been doing much better, but that didn't stop me from calling Andrea at all hours to come to my rescue when I felt myself slipping into my dark place. I'd always found it very difficult to ask for help in my life. But I felt broken, and I gave in to the support and comfort she always provided me.

In my self-absorbed state, I neglected to see the toll it was taking on her. Finally one day, she cracked.

"I can't do this anymore, Mom. I'm really sorry," she told me.

"I don't understand what you mean," I answered.

"This reliance on me has to stop. You have to find other ways to cope without always calling me to come to your rescue. I took a sabbatical from work and was there for you while Bob was sick, and it's been almost a year since he passed away. My family needs me now. I need me."

She told me this on the phone, and I was devastated. I'd always been proud of my independence and ability to cope during difficult situations in my life. But after Bob died, I felt needy, and I was embarrassed by my weakness. I also felt abandoned by my only daughter. It hurt so much to hear those words from her that I cried for two days. It didn't take me long, though, to realize she was right. Instead of relying on my own strength, I was like a vampire sucking the life out of her. Feelings of aloneness ached in my gut, and I wanted to cling to her like a life raft.

I looked at my tired face in the mirror. "You're stronger than this," I told myself. I knew I had to stop leaning on Andrea. It was time to let my daughter be my daughter, not my nursemaid.

Life seemed like a constant game of lost and found. I remembered a quote by Pema Chödrön: "To be fully alive, fully human, and completely awake is to be continually thrown out of the nest." I'd been thrown out of the nest so many times I needed a crash helmet. I'd rebuilt my life before, and I was determined to do it again.

+++

Andrea did the right thing by doling out some tough love to cut me loose. I needed to find a better way to cope on my own.

Forever thoughtful, Andrea gave me tools to help me help myself. She introduced me to *The Five Minute Journal* to help anchor my days with joy and gratitude. She taught me meditation techniques and breathing exercises to cope with my anxiety and gave me inspirational books by Richard Wagamese and Pema Chödrön to read. And through it all, Andrea was always loving and unwavering in her support. At times, I still felt like an abandoned child left at the door of an uncertain future. I had to fight the strong urge to melt into my sadness, and I longed for someone to take care of me. I thought I knew what grief was when I lost my father, my mother, and several dear relatives, but this was different. Losing both Estelle and Bob so close together was a crushing blow, and I wondered if I'd ever survive it.

Courage is a big thing in life. I think a lot of mine seeped away with Bob as I watched him fade into death. It was easier to give in and be needy and weak than to face my fears and move through them. After the life and career I'd had, I thought of myself as brave and capable. I clearly didn't like feeling that I'd failed the latest test of survival. I was desperate to move on with the time I had left in this world, but I wasn't exactly sure where to start. I desperately wanted to be back in charge.

I remembered one of the messages I often put in my bottles. It was a quote by Laird Hamilton: "Make sure your worst enemy is not living between your own two ears." I thought about those words and what they meant to me, and I wondered if I was my own worst enemy. I took a deep breath and decided to get out of my own way.

+++

I began to think about activities that might bring more happiness into my life and ways to challenge my comfort zone. I thought of the contentment I'd felt as a child, singing away the afternoons on my lawn swing. Music always had a way of lifting my spirits, so I considered joining a choir for the first time in my life. As I looked into it, I knew I didn't want the rigidity and music selections of more formal choirs. Then I found a pop choir, where the group sings more popular music, and that sounded like fun. I signed up for the weekly sessions and convinced a couple of friends to join me.

I met new people who loved to sing, and the choir experience was a glorious addition to my life. I was still creating my messages in a bottle, and sometimes I would scatter the bottles at the meetings and watch as people found them. They would look around for the source, and when they saw me watching, I simply shrugged. I found myself still singing and filled with joy as I headed to the parking lot after each choir meeting.

I also registered for an online course about the study of happiness offered by Yale University entitled The Science of Well-Being. I found the material and workshops fascinating. It taught me to be more aware of my surroundings and the little things in life: simple magical moments like stopping to enjoy the morning sun dancing on the water, or the curiosity of a small purple flower poking its head out of a garden of weeds, or the old-fashioned tip of the hat greeting offered by an older gentleman on my morning walk. Taking notice of these seemingly insignificant things made me feel lighter and more grateful for all the goodness in my life.

I was still meeting with my lovely girlfriends for our Saturday night card games, and I found myself looking forward to our gathering all week. It was an evening of companionship and laughter, and there was always lots of laughter. It was easier to hide my grief and dull my sorrow in the company of others.

I'd had a difficult time concentrating on reading when Bob was sick, but I began to enjoy books again. I'd organized the "Next Chapter Book Club" several years before, and now more than ever, I loved the company and support of this wonderful group of women. We all lived in my condo complex, and I knew I could count on every one of them for help if I asked. For the first time in my life, I understood the value of having women friends. I welcomed all the new sparks of joy lighting up my heart.

✦✦✦

At the end of September 2019, nine months after Bob's death, we held a beautiful memorial party for him. We filled Andrea's house with family and friends, pictures from Bob's life, great stories, delicious food, and wonderful music. Bob loved a good audience for his delicious sense of humour. He was a great joke teller, right down to the accents and physical manoeuvres that came with some of his hilarious stories. We toasted Bob, and everyone had a good laugh when my son-in-law, Sean, told Bob's best joke about a man in an ill-fitting suit. He mastered the timing and delivery, complete with comical contortions, just as my husband would have done.

Bob used to say he thought the perfect memorial gift when he died would be to give everyone an egg timer with his ashes in it. He had even contacted our lawyer many years before to ask if this could be done. The lawyer advised him it would be desecration of a body and not legal. So, at his memorial service, Sean told everyone about this wish of Bob's, and we handed out egg timers to everyone there although they were filled with sand and not Bob's remains. The following month, we buried his ashes in the Skene family plot at St. John's Norway Cemetery in Toronto. After the ceremony, I went home and fell asleep in Bob's lift chair, wrapped in his red heated blanket.

+++

All year, it felt as if I'd been trudging through miles and miles of sticky mud. Each time I thought I was free of it, it would suck me back deeper into the muck. But by November, I began to feel lighter in spirit and more content. The good news was that I was listening to holiday music instead of CNN. This was major progress for me.

This was going to be our first Christmas without Bob, and I knew it would be difficult. But we all got through it quite well by chasing away the heartaches with lots of good memories. I had a new ornament made with Bob's picture, and we gave it a place of honour on the tree. I slept at Andrea's on Christmas Eve because she didn't want me to wake up alone on Christmas morning.

During the night, I developed heart palpitations, which passed after a few hours. My heart doctor checked me out with a stress test a week later and said he was sure it was anxiety-induced. My heart was fine, he told me. But how could it be fine when it felt broken into a million pieces?

+++

The holidays ended, and January 8, 2020, soon arrived, marking the first anniversary of Bob's death. I was filled with memories, both good and bad. My chest felt heavy as I prepared dinner for Andrea, Farrell, and Sean, who would share this milestone with me. I placed a candle at Bob's place at the table.

Andrea told me Farrell was a bit nervous about coming, not sure what to expect. She and her Poppy had been very close, and she didn't talk much about him. Not to me anyway. She may have been worried she would make me cry. But I liked it when people talked about Bob; it held him present in our lives.

At dinner that night, we kept it light. I asked everyone to tell their funniest Bob story. My family loved the stories about how, for decades, I planned the perfect joke every April Fool's Day. Each year, Bob swore he wouldn't get caught again, but every year, I got him good. I often went to great lengths to make a plan, like the year I woke up early to paint my face to look like a scary Chucky doll from the movie. Then I crawled back into bed placing my face close to his and waited for him to wake up and see his hideous wife.

Bob left us with a lot of funny memories to share. It was easy to laugh and enjoy the flashbacks of better times and talk about how he influenced our lives. I felt so blessed and thankful for my wonderful family.

+++

The first year after Bob's death was over, and all the "firsts" were behind me. I took out a new batch of bottles and sat at my table looking out over the street. I thought about the many changes I'd been through over the past year. It had been a long painful journey, and I was finally beginning to feel a sense of peace. So much of me had healed since I first started preparing my bottles. So much time had passed since that dark windy day out on the Bronte pier.

+++

We all have the power to touch the lives of others and spread goodness, even in small ways. I won't know what impact I've made with my messages, if any, but the ripple effect of kindness can go deep. A smile directed at a stranger, a compliment given to a friend, or finding a mysterious little message in a bottle could become the best part of someone's day. I believe that everything we say and do has a life of its own. My little bottles helped me to matter, to feel a part of something bigger than myself. The ritual of making them gave structure to my days and helped me feel a sense of control and continuity. I wondered if I'd be sneaking into places for the rest of my life, leaving cryptic notes for strangers like some eccentric old lady. Who knew something so simple could bring me such joy and help to ground me when I felt rudderless in an ever-changing world?

But in March 2020, I was forced to stop my bottle project as the whole world was turned upside down with the COVID-19 virus.

CHAPTER 26

What Took You So Long?

By the summer of 2021, we were into our second year of a global pandemic with millions sick and dead around the world. I found it hard to watch the non-stop news reports of the devastating effects on families, businesses, and personal freedoms. I spent my last two birthdays alone. Andrea and her family included me in their bubble, but there were often times when it was safer to stay away from one another. The vaccines were being rolled out, and we were hopeful for some relief in the coming months.

I was thankful to have already experienced the initial growing pains of learning to live alone. The isolation that subsequently came with the pandemic was certainly an immersion into surviving solo. There were times in the early days of the pandemic when I thought I'd never make it. But as time went on, I found myself embracing the solitude and being grateful for my new feelings of contentment. I accepted the isolation as a reward for my safety and that of my family and friends. My heart ached for the people who died alone and their survivors who had to grieve alone. It was such a tragedy happening before our eyes.

Farrell graduated from high school a few months after the pandemic started. There was no official ceremony because gatherings weren't safe, so we had a small celebration at home. For her graduation gift, I gave her a sterling silver compass from Tiffany, inscribed with "Always head true north." That September, Farrell began her first year at Queen's University in Kingston. Farrell is a strong and intensely principled young woman with her whole life ahead of her. I hoped the words inscribed on the compass would be a guide to help her stay on the right path to follow her dreams and find her way home when she needs grounding. Going back to Britt and the Magnetawan River has always been my "true north," my fixed point on the globe that anchors me to who I am. I hoped Farrell would always stay true to who she is at her deepest level.

When the pandemic was raging on and we became even more isolated, Andrea invited me to stay with them so that I wouldn't be alone. But I resisted the urge to accept because I'd come so far and didn't want to slip back into that needy person again. I was coping well and filled my days with things I loved to do. My choir meetings had to stop, but I learned how to Zoom and set up the members of my book club to continue our monthly meetings. I played online euchre with my card group of friends to stay in touch. I enjoyed my early morning walks more than ever, read many great books, and maintained my daily yoga routine. And I began to write this memoir, sorting through my memories like a story shucker, removing the outer layers to dig for the juicy bits inside.

I relived my life on these pages and saw how I left the bubble of smallness and fought hard to open up the spaces around me. It wasn't always easy, and I didn't always fill the spaces with the right things. Sometimes, I was slow getting there, but I made it.

I'm grateful for the richness of all the events in my life, the good, the bad, and the unbearable. Many experiences have gone full circle with parts of my life needing resolution, like reclaiming my Métis heritage. Looking back, I find it interesting how I've been drawn to cultural reminders of my origins without questioning why: my love for storytelling, sweetgrass, smudging, Indigenous art, and the beautiful Ojibwe porcupine quill boxes I've collected over the years. Being immersed in nature, feeling the love of the land and water, has always been my happy place.

As time picks up speed in my older years, I still go back to my hometown of Britt for rejuvenation and grounding. The swiftly flowing waters of the Magnetawan River have become a metaphor for my life. The river has numerous rocky rapids along the route on its way to Georgian Bay. Like my journey, sometimes the currents move too swiftly and become overwhelming. But despite the obstacles and changing conditions, the river teaches me to keep moving forward. Rewinding and going backwards isn't an option.

Bob's death was devastating, but I finally found peace in knowing I helped him through his darkest days. He left this world on his own terms in his own bed wearing his Marvel Comics underwear with time to have a champagne toast and say goodbye to his family. Now, instead of the painful uncertainty of remorse that plagued me after witnessing his death, I finally feel relief in knowing that I did the right thing in helping him carry out his last wishes. I will be forever grateful that Canada's medical assistance in dying laws empowered my husband to die on his own terms. MAID was a beautiful and peaceful end of life for him and for our family. I feel honoured to have shared an incredible moment with him.

Remembering

When I'm lost, I close my eyes
To touch you in my mind,
And ask your help to guide my way
In dreams and quiet times.
We were special, you and I,
With sunshine in our song,
And when I hold your memory
My loneliness is gone.
We shared our lives together,
The music and the pain.
Although your time of rest has come,
Your strength and love remain.

So, every time I think of you,
Your spirit strong and free,
You feed the happy in my heart,
With all you were to me.

Despite living in a paralyzing world of virus turmoil, I've managed to find my centre of gravity. All the enforced isolation and time for reflection was a master class in self-reliance and healing. I'm content with the crooked path I've been on and the jagged peaks and valleys of my life. After learning to grow around my wounds, I squeeze the juice out of every day. I laugh more, cry when I feel like it, and embrace my new life with gratitude. I've even given away Bob's electric lift chair to Maureen and Dave for their cottage. I don't need it anymore. The Métis grandmother in the mirror is smiling, and that makes me smile back.

"So, what took you so long?" you might ask as others have done in my life. My answer is the title of a book I read by Barbara Gordon, published in 1979: *I'm Dancing as Fast as I Can*. I wasn't a perfect mother, I wasn't a perfect wife, and I'm nowhere near a perfect person. After being programmed at a very young age to deny my identity, I struggled with acceptance and self-worth my whole life. At every challenge along the way, I may have arrived late, frightened, and vulnerable, but I showed up and did the best I could. All in all, it sure hasn't been boring, and I'd do it all again to feel the contentment I do today.

I'll always love that spunky little Métis kid who set bushfires and slid down coal dumps in the rail yard. I was never looking to forget her. I just opened her cage, and she taught me how to fly. It took me more than seven decades to arrive at this place, and I feel like I've finally made it. I may not be at the highest point on the corporate ladder or an author on the best-seller list or a memorable human who will make it into the history books. But I'm an ordinary woman who stretched herself to face life's challenges and is at peace with knowing and accepting who she is. Anything less would be disrespectful to how I got here. It's been quite a ride! What took me so long, indeed!

EPILOGUE

I'm not sure how, or if, my life would have been different if my family had accepted our heritage and openly discussed who we were. Unlike my sister Estelle, I looked, behaved, and was treated as if I were a white woman. All I know is that when I finally embraced my Métis identity, I felt different. The empty corners of me had been filled with something good that belonged there. As sure as the handcrafted artistry of my Ojibwe quill boxes had always carried a silent message of recognition and connection, I knew this was who I was.

My niece Jessica is the principal of Indigenous education for a school board in Ontario. She is well connected in the Indigenous community because of her work. She was the first to take an active interest in tracing our roots and did the genealogy legwork that was necessary to get her Métis citizenship. Once the links were established that connected our family to two Métis root ancestors, it was easier for the rest of us to apply. Andrea and Farrell received their Métis status, and to complete the generational circle in my family, I became an official Métis citizen as well.

Farrell got a summer job with the Métis Nation of Ontario. She learned several Métis crafts, including dot art, beadwork, and finger weaving, and held online workshops to teach these Indigenous crafts to adults and children. We all felt proud to acknowledge the rich heritage of our ancestors.

Over the last few years, I've taken online courses and devoured books about Indigenous history and the Métis. Time and time again, I found myself in the pages of someone else's history, where the stories of Métis women my age were my stories too. Despite my efforts to acknowledge and embrace my indigeneity, I still experience some psychological slippage now and then. Part of me is still hard-wired to believe I'm someone else. Recently, I asked Jessica to connect me with a Métis grandmother for research on an Indigenous children's story I was writing. There was a long pause, and she finally said, "But Aunt Pat – that's you!"

"No," I said, "I mean someone who grew up in a Métis household. I'd like to interview someone who knows what it's like to be Métis as a child."

She laughed and said even louder, "But that's you! Think of the food you ate, where you lived, your connection to the water, the land, the music. Being Métis is the way you lived, even if no one talked about it."

When I stopped laughing at myself, I knew I had some residual deprogramming to do. I still need reminding, and even better if it comes from the next generation. The emerging news stories about missing Indigenous children break my heart as I think of my ancestors and what they may have been through. I feel a deep sadness that so much of my own history was buried in fear.

The pandemic is over, but my message-in-a-bottle project is still on hold, and I'm content to leave it that way. I believe the need has passed. But I found myself wondering again about the lives of the women who picked up my bottles. Yes, I imagined only women would be attracted to a small bottle tied with a bright ribbon and be curious enough to look inside. I began to create stories of old women, young women, and girls, ages twelve to eighty-seven years old, who might have found my bottles. I wrote eight "Message in a Bottle" stories in all, and they were published by the *Oakville News*, a digital news outlet where I live.

I didn't have a television or telephone in my early childhood, but I've come a long way since then. As I move on with my life, I'm hooked on anything with an Apple logo on it, and I embrace new technology innovations with the anticipation and thrill of a teenage kiss. I am still a fully connected senior with a tablet, a cellphone, a computer, and even a robot vacuum cleaner. I have a smartwatch with a feature that alerts my emergency contacts and calls 911 if I have a fall. And I use YouTube videos to learn how to set up all my own electronics and television programming. I have finally turned off CNN, and I'm happy to welcome the lazy yawn of silence in my home. I shop online for most things I need, including furniture, clothing, housewares, and groceries — another giant leap from the Simpson's and Eaton's catalogues I devoured as a child. One of my favourite pastimes is playing online Scrabble and chatting with people from around the globe. It feels good to connect with so many cyber pen pals.

All this new technology really gives me newfound energy. At my age, that's got to be worth something. As I grow older, I'm learning how to embrace change and enjoy it. It means I can stay current and talk about these innovations with my family and be part of their world. In some small way, it helps me feel relevant. The wonders of the Internet connect me with the universe, right from the comfort of my recliner.

I'm still writing, thankful for the opportunity to fill my days with a passion that is both energizing and healing. My new picture book, *Lights Along the River* (Orca Book Publishers, 2024), is about the day electricity came to my hometown of Britt in 1952. It gives children an inside look at what life was like before all the gizmos and gadgets they have today.

Yes, I've come a long way from living with gas-powered washing machines, wood stoves, and hand-cranked record players. In my sepia-drenched memories, those days seem like they were a part of a kinder, gentler life. But I was a child, and I didn't have to haul the water, chop the wood, or wrestle the frozen sheets off the clothesline.

It's incredible how much change we absorb in a lifetime, and the pace seems to quicken with every generation. It's nothing short of amazing! We all need to be amazed now and then to help smooth out the wrinkly bits.

Looking back on my life, I finally understand why surviving on my own has been one of the most challenging things I've ever done. I get why driving through Rogers Pass at thirty-two years old to cross from one life to another has stayed with me all these years.

Today, I love living alone. I no longer feel the teeth of anxiety in an empty home without my husband; I feel empowered, free, and capable. I still suffer from the occasional lupus flare-up, and I haven't been in the sun for more than thirty years. I'm good with that. I've learned there are worse things than living without sunlight on my skin. Of course, I sometimes get lonely and miss my sweetheart and the way he made me laugh and feel safe. I've never regretted my bold move of asking him for a date when we met. I'll always miss my epic chats with my sister Estelle and the loving friendship we shared for sixty-nine years. Both my husband and my sister took a big part of me with them when they died, but they also left so much of themselves behind. I hope they're together telling jokes and toasting the rest of us who loved them.

For the first time in my seventy-odd years, I do not have a male love interest in my life. At age five, I got my first kiss (on the cheek) from a boy, and I've always had some sort of love/crush interest since then. While I enjoy the company of men, I find it liberating to finally be a self-contained unit of independence.

I'm thankful for my beloved Andrea and Farrell, who are everything to me. Farrell is in her fourth year at Queen's University, and we have a special relationship. My daughter is always close by and remains my best friend and champion. I have my challenges as I'm thrust toward my octogenarian years. I get my share of occasional health issues that rattle me and knock me about. But I'm feeling more grounded and better equipped to find my way through them. I'm learning to trust myself and be patient as I live my way into the future.

I don't have all the answers, and I'm still learning how to ask the right questions. Writing my story makes me see my life through a different lens and has brought me closer to my ancestors. I've read that "healing is about peeling," and I guess that's what I'm doing. I continue to navigate my indigeneity, but I embrace every new discovery with gratitude. I now self-identify as Métis and have added my family surname of Lamondin to my name as the pieces of me come together. Thankfully, we can outwardly express our historic Indigenous roots because society is more tolerant now. I'm hopeful that by telling my story, other Métis writers will come forward and tell theirs. Together, we can help to debunk the kinds of Indigenous stereotypes many of us grew up believing.

As for always being thirty-two in my dreams, when I finished writing my story, something changed. Now when I dream, I'm no longer thirty-two; I am the age I am today. I'll miss seeing my younger self, frozen in time when I dream. But I'm happy that somewhere between the lines of this book, that young woman who crossed the Rocky Mountains so long ago found the courage to set herself free.

(From left side, top to bottom) My parents, Bill Lamondin and Laura Charron, before they were married, circa 1940. Me with my grandfather, Louis Lamondin, 1947. Me, my brother Bruce, and sister Estelle, 1950. My youngest sister, Maureen, with my aunt Bernice, Dad's sister, 1957. Me at my "dreaming age" of 32. I had just driven home from British Columbia in 1977.
My daughter, Andrea, Bob, and I. Our New Year's Eve Wedding, 1982. Photos are courtesy of the author.